Doune Food

Celebrating
25 years of
Doune Dining Room

Liz Tibbetts

for Alan and Mary

nigiro
tea

contents

about Doune food

When we first opened, we made a conscious decision to use the words dining room and not restaurant. The most important thing was that we were catering for our own guests, most of whom are here for a whole week, and right from the start we put a lot of time into menu planning. We cook the same meal for everyone in the Dining Room and the balance between finding unusual flavours without being too 'out there' is an ongoing challenge. Taste, colour, texture, seasonality and local specialities are all taken into account. The aim is for each dish to be spot on, that it works within a perfectly balanced menu and that the menus for the whole week build up to a great overall experience.

I think there is a need for a return to real home cooking and Doune food is just that, all be it scaled up a bit. The recipes may change but our ethos on food hasn't altered at all. We still make everything from scratch ourselves and use the best ingredients we can find. Many of these are locally produced, with fruits, salads, edible flowers and herbs still coming from our Doune gardens. We also continue to do a set menu and 'family service'. Our guests frequently tell us how relaxing it is being presented with a lovely meal without the stress of choosing from a complicated menu, and that's all part of a holiday at Doune.

I have tried to remember the origin of all the recipes and where appropriate give a credit. Many have come from our guests, as over the years when we have given away recipes we have asked for one in return. Most are not used verbatim but the essence is there even if a certain amount of tweaking has gone on. The same process happens when we try our own ideas, and it never stops as we hone them over time to be the best possible version.

The link between all the recipes here is that we have served them at Doune, and it makes for a diverse and eclectic mix. We have had so much fun in the kitchen over the years and I hope you will too as you browse through the book and try some of the recipes.

Happy Doune cooking!

Liz

Starters

Among our many starters, we serve fresh crab every week; it has become a speciality of the house. Jane has done an amazing job being in charge of crab catching for many years. (A task not for the faint hearted!) With boiling and then careful picking to be done the whole process is a labour of love.

Beetroot and Halloumi Salad

As with all beetroot recipes, this is best at the end of the summer when the new season beets are brilliantly coloured and full of juice. The ratio of ingredients can be varied, and extra Halloumi would make it into a substantial main course. We have also made it very successfully with roast butternut squash.

serves 6
450g / 1lb fresh beetroot
1 tbs olive oil
1 soft leaf lettuce
½ to 1 packet Halloumi cheese
½ tablespoon olive oil
1 large crisp eating apple, washed.
a few fresh mint leaves, finely chopped
for the dressing:
2 tbs white wine vinegar
4 tbs olive oil
1 tsp lemon juice
½ tsp brown sugar
½ tsp runny honey
1 tsp Dijon mustard

Preheat the oven to 200°C / gas mark 6. Peel the beetroot and cut into large chunks, roast in the olive oil for about half an hour or until soft. Cool, cut up into smaller dice, place in a bowl, cover, and keep until ready to serve. Wash the lettuce, wrap it in a tea towel and tie the ends, go outside and fling it around your head for a few times to get rid of the excess water. Put the whole thing in the fridge until ready to serve; this will crisp it up nicely. Dice the Halloumi and leave to drain. Shake all the dressing ingredients together in a jar. When ready to serve, lay the salad leaves onto a serving dish and sprinkle the beetroot over them. Carefully fry the Halloumi in the remaining olive oil, turning once so it is browned on two sides and then lift out onto kitchen paper to drain. Core and dice the apple and sprinkle over the salad. Give the dressing a final shake and drizzle sparingly over the salad. Top off with the warm Halloumi, sprinkle with a little mint and serve immediately.

Cashew Nut Pâté

This is rich and delicious. We often serve it as a vegetarian option and it also makes an unusual sandwich filling.

serves 4
85g / 3oz raw cashew nuts
175g / 6oz vegetarian cream cheese
1 carrot, grated
1 tbs chopped fresh parsley
salt and freshly ground black pepper
1 tbs natural yoghurt

Toast the cashew nuts in a dry frying pan, stirring continuously, until they are taking on a little colour. Cool and grind in a food processor so that they are mostly fine but still have some texture. Beat everything together and serve with plenty of fresh green salad.

Smoked Salmon Blinis

This is such a pretty starter and easy to serve as everything can be made in advance. (If you do this, warm the blinis very slightly in the oven just to refresh them before assembling.) We sometimes use the same topping and salmon roses on herbed potato rosti. Follow the method for making our breakfast hash browns but make them bigger and add some chopped chives, dill and melted butter to the potato before frying. These do have to be cooked at the last minute, but they are seriously good.

serves 6

50g / 2oz buckwheat flour
110g/ 4oz strong white flour
pinch salt
1 tsp dried yeast
85ml / 3 fl oz crème fraîche
85ml / 3 fl oz milk
1 egg, separated
butter for frying

for the topping:

6 dsp crème fraîche
1 tsp Dijon mustard
fresh chopped dill to taste
finely snipped chives to taste
salt and pepper to taste
6 large slices of smoked salmon
extra dill and chives to serve

Sieve the flours together into a bowl and add the salt and yeast. Gently warm the crème fraîche and milk so it is warm to the touch and beat in the egg yolks. Mix the liquid into the flour and beat until smooth. Cover and leave in a warm place for about an hour. When bubbling nicely, whisk the egg whites until stiff and fold them into the mixture. Cook 2 or 3 at a time using two large tablespoons of batter per blini, it should make 6. Smear butter onto your pan and fry at quite a high temperature so they cook quickly, turning once. Cool on a rack.
Cut the smoked salmon into strips about 3cm / 1¼ in wide and roll up to form 6 rosettes of smoked salmon, cover lightly and leave in the fridge until ready to serve. Beat all the topping ingredients together. To serve, place a dessert spoon of the crème fraîche mixture on to each blini and top with a smoked salmon rose. Sprinkle with herbs.

Smoked Paprika Pâté

A lovely vegetarian starter, leave out the yoghurt for a stiffer mix to make a delicious sandwich filling.

serves 6

4 large cloves roasted garlic
350g / 12oz vegetarian cream cheese
12 marinated sun-dried tomatoes, drained and chopped
½ to ¾ tsp smoked paprika
salt and freshly ground pepper
1 tsp chopped fresh oregano or a good pinch of dried
1 tbs natural yoghurt

Squeeze the roast garlic out of its skins and mash with a fork against the side of a bowl. Mix in the rest and taste. For a starter, serve with green salad and fresh tomatoes.

Spicy Leaf Salads

We serve a variety of salad starters with a base of spicy leaves. They are light and tasty and a good way to use some of the more unusual salad leaves that we grow ourselves. Edible flowers, especially nasturtium, make a stunning garnish. If you can't find watercress and rocket separately, a couple of bags of spicy salad mix is a good substitute. It is really special if you can grow it all yourself!

serves 6
1 bag watercress
1 bag rocket
any other spicy leaves such as nasturtium, mizuna, mustard, golden frill, dragon's breath etc.
edible flowers to garnish
something on top as the main event with a salad or dressing to suit, see any of the variations below
Wash the salad leaves, place in a clean tea towel and shake well. Tie up the towel and refrigerate for a few hours to get really crisp.

<u>Hot Smoked Salmon</u>
We have recently started smoking our own hot smoked salmon and I'm not sure why it has taken us so long. It is a revelation. Of course, the bought product is pretty good too!
Allow **40g / 1½ oz per portion**. Flake carefully and layer on top of the salad. The following <u>remoulade</u> is nice and sharp to counter the richness of the fish:
9 cornichons, finely chopped
18 capers, finely chopped
¼ medium red onion, diced very fine
juice ½ lemon
black pepper
1 tbs fresh chopped dill
2 tbs mayonnaise
Mix all together, cover and chill for a few hours to meld. A gentle pink colour comes out of the red onion and it is really pretty with the salmon.

<u>Smoked Cod's Roe</u>
350g / 12oz smoked cod's roe
juice ½ lemon
1 tbs olive oil
1 clove garlic, crushed
150 ml / ¼ pint fresh double cream

Blend everything together until light and fluffy. Serve in a dish surrounded by the spicy salad leaves.

Venison Salami
Very thinly sliced really good quality air-dried venison or pork salami. Allow **25g / 1oz per person**.
Serve with tzatziki (page 19) or this celeriac relish:
½ small celeriac, peeled and grated
1 green apple, peeled and grated
juice ½ lemon, mixed with the apple
natural yoghurt to make a soft consistency.

Smoked Venison
Use **25g / 1oz per portion** and form it into an individual rose. Again, tzatziki or the celeriac relish above are ideal to balance the saltiness.

Pear and Walnut
A delicious sweet and sour combination.
6 truly ripe pears, peeled and cut into chunks
juice ½ lemon
1 tsp sugar
1 tbs extra virgin olive oil
50g / 2oz broken walnuts, sieved to remove dust
25g / 1oz freshly grated Parmesan
25g / 1oz fresh Parmesan in a block
Mix the pears with the lemon juice and sugar and leave for a few minutes for the juices to run. Place the salad leaves on a platter. Strain off the juice, whisk it with the olive oil and drizzle over the salad.
Top with the pear chunks, sprinkle with the walnuts and grated Parmesan and decorate with shavings of Parmesan from the block.

Smoked Venison Pâté

I invented this one year when our home-smoked venison was not as successful as usual and we had lots of broken bits to use up. I know most people won't have access to such bounty but I'm sure it could be made with any smoked meat and be just as good. You could also vary the proportion of roast meat to smoked.

serves 10

85g / 3oz cold roast venison or beef
175g / 6oz smoked venison bits
225g / 8oz pork mince
50g / 2oz butter
110g / 4oz chicken livers
1 clove garlic, crushed
1 tbs whisky
½ red pepper, de-seeded
½ green pepper, de-seeded
½ yellow pepper, de-seeded
½ tsp dried thyme
½ tsp red peppercorns, crushed
½ tsp juniper berries, crushed
1 egg, beaten
140ml / ¼ pint double cream

Trim the roast meat very carefully for skin and gristle and place in a food processor. Process until well chopped. Add the smoked venison and pork mince and process again. Melt the butter in a pan and brush some around an ovenproof dish or standard 900g / 2lb loaf tin. Trim the chicken livers and roughly chop. Fry very lightly with the garlic in the rest of the butter, add the whisky, bubble, and add to the processor. Process all until almost smooth but some texture remaining. Turn into a large bowl. Preheat the oven to 180°C / gas mark 4. Chop the peppers into 1½ cm / ½ inch dice and add to the bowl with all the other ingredients. Mix well and press lightly into your prepared dish or tin. Cover with foil, bake for half an hour then reduce to 150°C / gas mark 2 for 1 hour. When cooked it will have pulled away from the sides a little (if you have a probe it needs to be 75°C in the middle). Cook a little longer if required. Cool, chill well, turn out and surround with a crisp lettuce and mixed pepper salad drizzled with classic dressing.

Nut Pâté

Mary and I used to use this Cranks, (one of the original vegetarian restaurants in London), recipe as a nut roast for vegetarians when we did a roast. Then we discovered that the leftovers were really good cold for lunch and turned it into a starter which has been a huge favourite over the years. We use a much higher proportion of peanuts to other nuts.

serves 8

1 onion, finely chopped
1 tbs olive oil
110g / 4oz fresh white breadcrumbs
225g / 8oz mixed nuts: raw peanuts, brazils, hazels
1 tsp mixed dried herbs
1 tsp Marmite

300ml / just over ½ pint boiling water
freshly ground black pepper

Fry the onion in the oil until soft and slightly brown. Dissolve the Marmite in the boiling water. Chop the nuts in a food processor carefully so they are quite coarse, remove half of them and chop the rest so they are really fine. (Use the same strategy if you are using a knife to chop but it takes a lot longer!). Preheat the oven to 180°C / gas mark 4. Mix everything together to make a soft mixture, adding a little more water if needed. Turn into an oiled flattish dish so the mixture is about 3cm / 1¼ in deep. Cover with foil and bake at 180°C / gas mark 4 for 15 minutes. Remove the foil and bake a further 5 minutes. Cool. Turn out onto a serving platter, if it doesn't come out cleanly don't worry, you can stick it back together! If not serving straight away, cover with cling film to avoid the surface drying out. We like to garnish with lettuce, herb leaves, slithers of red pepper and slices of button mushroom. Serve with a French dressing or mayonnaise.

Scallops and Bacon

This recipe was given to me by one of our guests. Scallops are rich and filling even without this amazing sauce so with just a few extra scallops this makes a great main course with waxy new potatoes and some fresh green salad. As a starter, I try to pair it with a lighter main course.

serves 6
2 slices streaky bacon, preferably dry cured
3 cloves garlic
9 large hand-dived scallops, shucked
280ml / ½ pint dry white wine
1½ tbs double cream
seasoning to taste
1 tsp chopped fresh parsley
1 tsp chopped fresh thyme

Chop the bacon and dry fry slowly in a heavy-based frying pan. Add the garlic once some fat has come out of the bacon and continue until the bacon is very crisp. Remove, drain well and keep warm. Slice the scallops in half to make thin discs. Fry briefly in the bacon fat until their translucence is just gone, turning once. Remove, drain well and keep warm. Pour off any excess bacon fat, just leaving a little in the pan. Add the wine and bubble to reduce by half. Add the cream and taste and season. Place the scallops in your serving dish and scatter on the bacon. Add the herbs to the sauce and pour it over the scallops to serve.

Avocado and Mint Starter

This was one of my own ideas, it is light and summery, and the lemon cuts the richness of the avocado. Fresh mint is a must and one of the sweeter varieties is best. We grow several and my favourite for this is Tashkent mint or, for a close second, young leaves of apple mint (the bigger leaves can get rather coarse).

serves 6

1 lemon, juice only
caster sugar to just sweeten the juice
225g / 8oz black grapes
225g / 8oz green grapes
3 ripe avocados
fresh garden mint
sprigs of mint to garnish

Juice the lemon and stir in a little sugar to dissolve, taste and add more if necessary. You need to take the edge off the lemon without making it sweet. Wash and halve the grapes. Halve and stone the avocados, cut into chunky dice and scrape out of the skin, keeping the chunks as neat as possible. Chop the mint, you will need a small handful. Carefully mix the avocado, grapes, lemon juice and some of the mint. Taste and add more mint if you want. Pile onto plates and garnish with sprigs of mint. It looks lovely on a dark plate.

Kipper Pâté

Mallaig has been famous for its kippers since the 1920's and we love to use this superb local product. We offer them as an occasional extra at breakfast and make this unusual pâté.

serves 6 to 8

3 large whole kippers
175g / 6oz fresh white breadcrumbs
zest and juice 1 lemon
2 tbs fresh chopped parsley
freshly ground black pepper (no salt)
110ml / 4 fl oz double cream
1 egg, beaten

Gently poach the kippers in water to just cover. Remove, cool, and skin and bone. Preheat the oven to 180°C / gas mark 4. Blend the flesh in a food processor (or mash with a fork) and mix with the rest of the ingredients except for half the lemon juice. Add water to make a soft consistency. Turn into a greased flattish dish so the mixture is about 3cm / 1¼ in deep. Cover with foil and bake for 20 minutes. Remove the foil and bake a further 5 minutes; it should still be soft. Turn out immediately and drizzle over the rest of the lemon juice. Cover tightly with cling film to prevent it drying out while cooling. Serve with lots of fresh green salad including fresh sorrel and flat leaf parsley if you can.

Mezze Platter with Focaccia

The ultimate sharing starter with the ultimate sharing bread. These days there are plenty of wonderful bakery Focaccia to buy, and that is fine, but if you want to make your own I don't think you can improve on the version by James Morton. It's not the most traditional, but it has bags of character, is loads of fun, and is the one we make. Check out his YouTube video and see how he copes with the fiendishly tricky wet dough. You could, of course, use any Focaccia recipe or even our bread roll recipe and make it into a delicious flat loaf drizzled with olive oil and sprinkled with flaked sea salt and fresh rosemary. We try to keep our selection of mezze as light as possible and the best time is the height of the summer when the garden has produced loads of cherry tomatoes, courgettes, cucumbers and fresh basil. Here are some ideas.

Ordinary supermarket **olives** marinaded for a few days in garlic, oregano, rosemary, bay leaves and olive oil.
Very thinly sliced **good quality salami or smoked meat.**
Slow roast cherry tomatoes, cut in half, drizzle with olive oil and sprinkle with equal salt and sugar mix and fresh thyme. Bake on the bottom shelf for 1 hour at 150°C / gas mark 2 then reduce to 100°C / gas mark ¼ for another hour or two until they are slightly dried out.
Courgettes in thin strips, tossed in lemon juice and seasoning and mixed with fresh torn basil leaves.
Home-made **tzatziki**, see our roast pepper salad recipe on page 19.
Home-made **taramasalata**, 225g / 8oz salt or smoked fish roe, ½ small onion, 110g / 4oz stale white crustless bread, juice 1 lemon, 200ml / 7 fl oz extra virgin olive oil, black pepper. If the roe is very strongly smoked, scoop it out of its skin and soak in cold water for a couple of hours. Drain well before use. Put the bread in cold water, then drain immediately and squeeze out the excess. Blend everything together until smooth.
Dipping dishes of **chilli oil** (we keep a jar of olive oil with chopped chillies and garlic at the ready) and **olive oil with balsamic vinegar**.
Garnish with **edible flowers.**

Herb Terrine

We have a general rule that recipes are straightforward with as little faff as possible but this is definitely an exception. Anne-Marie (who was with us for four years in the early 2000's) used to announce to the dining room that there are 25 ingredients in this and it took all morning to make; she was not far wrong. It was my attempt at recreating a pâté that Andy and I enjoyed at Robert Carrier's restaurant when we got engaged, rather a long time ago! We don't make it so often these days but I do try to fit it in a couple of times a season. The recipe makes a lot but it is not worth the effort to make less and it freezes well.

serves about 20
450g / 1lb minced pork
25g / 1oz butter
1 large onion, chopped
2 cloves garlic, crushed
450g / 1lb spinach
225g / 8oz chicken livers
25g / 1oz butter
110g / 4oz cooked ham, cubed
110g / 4oz cooked chicken, cubed
110g / 4oz cooked tongue, cubed (or more chicken/ham)
2 tbs fresh basil
2 tbs fresh parsley
2 tbs fresh dill, tarragon or chervil
24 spikes fresh rosemary
4 eggs beaten
pinch cayenne pepper
freshly grated nutmeg
salt and freshly ground black pepper
140ml / ¼ pint double cream
8 sheets leaf gelatin, soaked then dissolved in 2 tbs hot water
110g to 175g / 4oz to 6oz streaky bacon

Blend the pork mince in a food processor. Fry the onion and garlic in the butter and add the spinach to wilt it. Add this to the processor, blend again and turn into a large bowl. Briefly fry the chicken livers in more butter, process and add to the bowl. Add the cubes of meat, finely chopped herbs, eggs, spices and seasoning. Stir in the cream and dissolved gelatin. Fry a teaspoon of the mixture to check the seasoning and adjust if needed, remember the bacon will add some saltiness. Preheat the oven to 170°C / gas mark 3. Line 2 standard 900g / 2lb loaf tins with greaseproof paper. Stretch the bacon with the back of a knife so that it is very thin, and lay strips across the width of the tins. Spoon in the mixture and fold any overhanging bacon over the top. Cover with foil and bake for 30 minutes then reduce the temperature to 150 °C / gas mark 2 and cook a further 40 to 45 minutes. A probe is useful to check that it is cooked enough; it should read 75°C in the middle. Cool in the tin and chill well before turning out. Serve whole or in slices with a green salad garnish, a drizzle of French dressing and lots of fresh herbs to garnish.

Roast Pepper Salad

We use this as a light starter before a roast but it would also be great as a lunch dish. Perfect for the summer when peppers and tomatoes are at their best. Instead of tzatziki we sometimes use hummus, thinned with a little more olive oil and some water so it will drizzle, and sprinkled with fresh oregano, or thyme.

serves 8
2 large red peppers
2 large yellow peppers
olive oil and seasoning
1 punnet cherry tomatoes
1 large soft leaf lettuce
<u>for the tzatziki dressing:</u>
½ medium cucumber
½ tsp salt
250g / 9oz Greek yoghurt
1 clove garlic, crushed
juice ½ lemon
1 tbs fresh mint leaves, chopped

Start with the dressing: Dice the cucumber very fine and mix in the salt. Put in a plastic sieve and allow to drain for a couple of hours. Rinse and drain again then mix with the rest of the dressing ingredients. Preheat the oven to 190°C / gas mark 5. Cut the peppers into strips and roast in olive oil and seasoning for 30 minutes or so until soft and a bit caramelised at the edges. Halve the tomatoes, add to the mix and roast for 5 more minutes only. Remove, drain, and cool. Wash the salad leaves, shake, wrap in a clean tea towel and refrigerate. When ready to serve, make a base of the salad leaves, arrange the roast vegetables and drizzle the dressing over the top.

Onion Tart

This tart is adapted from a Delia Smith recipe. It is delicious with our Beetroot and Raspberry Salad on page 51. Individual tarts make a good vegetarian main course option; we make 6 out of this quantity.

serves 8
900g / 2lb onions, finely sliced
6 tbs balsamic vinegar
25g / 1oz butter
1 tbs chopped fresh sage (or 1 tsp dried)
our standard shortcrust pastry as on page 161, plus 50g / 2oz grated Cheddar cheese and a pinch of cayenne before mixing
225g / 8oz Brie cheese, sliced
fresh chopped parsley to garnish

Cook the onions, vinegar, butter and sage together for 30 minutes until the onions are meltingly soft. Preheat the oven to 180°C / gas mark 4. Use the pastry to line a 25.5cm / 10in shallow tart tin and bake for 20 minutes. To serve, preheat the grill, reheat the onions and spoon into the pastry case. Top with the Brie slices and grill to melt. Sprinkle with parsley and serve with the beetroot salad.

Tartiflette

Tartiflette is a bit time consuming to make but well worth the effort. For its flavour and melting properties, do use the traditional Reblochon cheese if you can get it, but if not, a ripe Brie or Camembert is still delicious. Quantities here are for a starter, just double up for a 'comfort food' main meal.

To make it vegetarian use a little butter for frying, then add chopped mushrooms instead of the bacon or chopped peppers and some smoked paprika. You will need to choose a cheese made with vegetarian rennet.

new potatoes cut into cubes, enough to well cover the bottom of your chosen dish.
smoked bacon (dry cured if possible) 1oz / 25g per person.
garlic 1 clove for 2 people.
onions 1 for 4 people.
salt and fresh ground pepper.
double cream to make the mixture nice and moist.
Reblochon or Brie or other soft rind cheese.

for the Walnut Dressing:

25ml / 1 fl oz white wine vinegar
75 ml / 3 fl oz walnut oil
1 tbs lemon juice
1 tsp brown sugar
1 tsp runny honey
2 tsp Dijon mustard

Choose a shallow heat-resistant serving dish. Parboil the potatoes until almost done. Sauté the bacon (without extra oil) over medium heat until slightly crispy and the fat has run out. Remove with a slotted spoon. In the bacon fat, sweat the onions and garlic until transparent. Preheat the oven to 180°C / gas mark 4. In a large bowl, toss everything together with plenty of seasoning and enough cream as needed to make the mixture quite moist. Pour into your serving dish, it should make a layer about 3cm / 1¼ inches thick. Bake for 10 to 15 minutes or until the cream is nicely bubbling. Allow to cool. To finish, cut knobs of the cheese and sprinkle over the top. Bake at 220°C / gas mark 7 for 10 to 15 minutes until golden. Allow to cool for a couple of minutes before eating. Serve with crisp salad lightly dressed with some walnut dressing.

Bagged

Watermelon and Feta Salad

A lovely refreshing salad, really welcome on a hot summer evening. It looks beautiful too. We sometimes vary this and use fresh chopped tarragon instead of the parsley and mint. Use about 2 tablespoons.

serves 6
½ to 1 watermelon, the skin and white layer cut off, cut into chunks.
small bunch flat leaf parsley, leaves only, slightly torn
1 to 2 tbs young apple mint leaves, finely chopped
85g / 3oz pitted black olives
juice 1 lime
175g / 6oz Feta cheese, cut into cubes

You need about 175g / 6oz prepared watermelon per person. Strain the chunks (if it is very ripe it will make a lot of juice). In a large bowl, mix all except the Feta together. Pile up on your serving plate placing cubes of Feta as you go. Garnish with whole parsley leaves and sprigs of mint.

Smoked Salmon Mousse

The simplest of recipes are often the best and this is one of them. Perennially popular we tend to serve it plain with our fresh bread rolls but it is also great as a filling for little choux buns or a savoury roulade. Not strictly a mousse, the whipped cream should be carefully folded in to make it light and fluffy.

serves 6
175g / 6oz smoked salmon
juice ½ lemon
350g / 12oz cream cheese
1 dsp mayonnaise
2 spring onions, chopped
1 tbs fresh chopped parsley
4 tbs whipped cream
freshly ground black pepper

Put the smoked salmon and lemon juice into a food processor and process until smooth. Add the cream cheese and mayonnaise and process until well mixed. Add the spring onions and parsley and pulse quickly to mix but not mash up the spring onion. Turn into a bowl and fold in the cream. Taste for seasoning, a little freshly ground black pepper is good but it will probably be salty enough. You may also like to add a little more lemon juice. Chill well before serving.

hummus

Hummus, or should the plural be hummi? Whichever, we seem to have lots of them! They suit our style perfectly: rustic, uber tasty and perfect with our freshly baked rolls. Many recipes use tinned chickpeas but if you want to use dried, 110g / 4oz will produce the same weight of cooked peas as one tin. Soak overnight with a good pinch of bicarbonate of soda and then boil for about twenty minutes until soft. We often use dried because we think the taste and texture is superior, especially for the traditional version.

Red Pepper Hummus

This was the first hummus variation we tried and it was so popular we were inspired to keep trying...

serves 8

1 large (or two small) red peppers, roasted
2 tins chickpeas, drained
1 tbs tahini
1 large clove garlic
1 tsp ground cumin
juice 1 lemon
2 tbs extra virgin olive oil
2 tsp paprika
salt to taste

Blend the red pepper first then add the rest. Add a little water to get a soft and fluffy consistency. Taste and add more flavourings if you like, it should be strong and zingy. Cover and leave to meld until serving. It goes well with the tomato salad for the traditional hummus (page 24) or lettuce with alfalfa or bean-sprouts.

Peanut Hummus

This is a slight variation of a recipe by Nigella Lawson. You can be more or less generous with the peanut butter to your taste.

serves 8

2 tins chickpeas, drained
1 clove garlic
3 tbs extra virgin olive oil
2 tbs peanut butter
juice 1 lemon
1 tsp salt
2 tsp ground cumin
3 tbs sour cream
water if needed

Blend everything together adding a little water if needed to make a soft and fluffy consistency. To serve, sprinkle with a few chopped roasted peanuts and some leaves of coriander or flat parsley. It is good with tomato and fresh coriander salad or any crunchy salad mixture, especially including cucumber.

Hummus with Tomato Salad

This recipe was given to me in my student days by a Greek student desperate for some food like his mum used to make. At the time, hummus wasn't readily available in the shops so once a month we would sneak into the hall kitchens and make up a batch to keep him from getting too homesick! He used to mash it with a potato masher and then beat it hard with a wooden spoon. These days, for the quantities we deal with, I wouldn't like to be without the food processor. Freshly boiled chickpeas rather than tinned give it a delicate, authentic flavour.

serves 6 to 8
225g / 8oz dried chickpeas, soaked and boiled, or two tins
zest and juice 1 lemon
1 tbs tahini
1 tbs good extra virgin olive oil
2 cloves garlic, crushed
salt
for the salad:
really ripe tomatoes
fresh basil, marjoram or coriander
sea salt flakes
freshly coarse ground black pepper
drizzle of extra virgin olive oil

Drain the chickpeas but reserve a little of the liquid. Blend everything together adding a little of the liquid to make a soft, fluffy consistency, not too coarse, not too smooth! Taste and add more garlic, lemon or salt as needed. Cover and leave to meld. Serve sprinkled with paprika, a drizzle of extra virgin olive oil and the tomato salad using whichever fresh herb is at its best.

Carrot and Cashew Nut Hummus

I had a yen to make a carrot hummus for a long time and after exhaustive testing, we decided on this delicious combination. It is set off perfectly by our carrot and cucumber salad with sweet chilli dressing (page 51). In this case we omit the red onion.

serves 6 to 8
450g / 1lb carrots
2 tbs extra virgin olive oil
3 large cloves garlic
1 level tsp coriander seeds
1 tin chickpeas, drained
1 tbs orange juice
½ tsp salt
2 dsp cashew nut butter

Preheat the oven to 200°C / gas mark 6. Peel the carrots, cut into chunks and place on a baking tray. Mix with one tablespoon of the olive oil, add the garlic cloves (still in their skins) and roast in the oven for about 40 minutes until the carrot is soft. In a dry frying pan, toast the coriander seeds for about a minute until fragrant, then cool and grind finely. Squeeze the garlic out of its skin. Put everything into a food processor, and blend until smooth and light, adding a little water if needed to get the consistency you like.

Harissa Hummus with Cabbage and Lime

This is the spicy option hummus. Just add more or less of the harissa paste to control the spice level. Making your own harissa paste is fun and gives a great result, but it is fine to use a bought paste. We make a large amount of paste and freeze it in ice cube trays. The cabbage and lime salad is surprisingly cooling against the heat of the harissa and also adds crunch.

serves 4 to 6
1 tin chickpeas, drained
1½ tbs sour cream
1 clove garlic
juice ½ lemon
¼ tsp salt
2 to 3 tsp harissa spice mix
1 tbs fresh chopped mint
1 to 3 tsp hot harissa paste
a little water to get the consistency you like
for the salad:
¼ small hard white cabbage
½ to 1 fresh lime, zest and juice
for the spice mix:
equal quantities of cumin seeds, coriander seeds and caraway seeds, gently toasted and ground
for the harissa paste:
50g / 2oz fresh hot chillies, 5 cloves garlic, 3 tbs olive oil, 1 tsp caraway seeds, 1 tsp cumin seeds, 1½ tsp salt, 4 tsp sugar, 1 tbs white wine vinegar, ½ inch ginger, 2 tsp dried mint, juice and rind 1 lemon, 1 tsp rose water, 1 large roasted red pepper. Grind the seeds, chop the chillies, garlic, ginger and pepper. Blend all together to make a paste.

Slice the white cabbage as thinly as you can. Mix in the lime zest and juice and leave in a cool place to meld while you make the hummus.
Blend all the hummus ingredients together. Add water as needed to make it light and soft. Taste and add any further flavourings as required.
Garnish with thin slices of fresh chilli and serve with the cabbage salad.

Pea and Mint Hummus with Quinoa Salad

This easy hummus is an amazing colour and has a fresh cool flavour. Other fresh soft leaf herbs also work well, as does a handful of watercress. Instead of the quinoa, couscous, bulghur wheat or other grains can be used with the same flavourings.

serves 6

1 can chickpeas, drained
1 clove garlic, crushed
juice 1 to 2 limes
1 tsp tahini
225g / 8oz fresh or frozen green peas, blanched and drained
1 tbs chopped fresh sweet mint (not peppermint)
1 tbs extra virgin olive oil
salt and freshly ground black pepper
<u>for the Quinoa:</u>
85g / 3oz red quinoa
½ tsp salt
280ml / ½ pint water
3 tomatoes (as red as possible), finely diced
1 tbs fresh chopped sweet mint
2 tbs fresh chopped parsley, flat leaf if possible
1 tbs extra virgin olive oil
juice ½ to 1 lemon
salt and freshly ground black pepper

Simmer the quinoa and salt in the water for 15 to 20 minutes until it is soft and has split. Cool, drain any excess water and mix in the rest of the salad ingredients. Blend all the hummus ingredients together. Taste and add any further herbs or seasoning as required.

Beetroot Hummus with Apple and Beet Relish

The first time we tried making beetroot hummus we didn't get the ratio of beet to chickpeas right and the colour was strange and unappetizing. This put us off for some time but when we decided to try it again, bingo, the colour was a vibrant pink (which was set off perfectly by fresh green salad leaves) and the flavour was amazing. Now we have found a sweet and sour apple relish to complement the earthy flavoured hummus - it's a great combination and adds more lovely colour.

serves 4 to 6

110g / 4oz fresh boiled and skinned beetroot
½ tsp cumin seeds, freshly roasted and ground
1 tin chickpeas, drained
1 tsp tahini
juice ½ lemon
¼ tsp salt
1 clove garlic, crushed
1 dsp extra virgin olive oil
a little water if needed

for the relish:

225g / 8oz peeled onions, chopped fine
350g / 12oz peeled and cored cooking apples, chopped small
240ml / 8 fl oz red wine vinegar
½ tsp salt
225g / 8oz fresh boiled and skinned beetroot, finely diced
2 tbs light soft brown sugar

Blend the beetroot in a food processor until as fine as possible. Add the rest of the ingredients and process until smooth. Add more water if required to make a smooth light hummus (it will depend on the juiciness of the beets). Taste and add seasoning as needed. Serve with the relish on a bed of fresh green salad leaves.

For the relish: Put the apples and onions in a pan with the vinegar and salt and simmer gently until soft. Add the beetroot and sugar and boil again to meld together. Pot in sterile jars while still warm. It makes 3 to 4 jars and keeps well. Use about a dessertspoon per portion.

Soups

Good soups come from good stock and we are lucky to have bones from our weekly roast to make superb rich bases for our meat soups. The longer they cook the better, we often put them in the oven at the same time as slow cooking casseroles and we make sure they get at least 6 hours simmering in total. We don't generally add vegetables or herbs to meat stocks, they are just pure meaty goodness. Our vegetable stock recipe is on page 32, crab on page 35, fish on page 38 and chicken on page 62.

Lovage Soup

We grow lots of lovage at Doune and use it in a number of recipes. Although very easy to grow, sadly it is very seasonal and is only at its best for a short time at the start of the summer. After that, it starts to die back and although we manage it so we can pick a little right through the summer it is rarely possible to make this soup outside the months of May, June or July.

serves 7 to 8

a big bunch of lovage
2 small onions, roughly chopped
40g / 1½ oz butter
1 clove garlic, crushed
8 small pieces of peeled floury potato
850ml / 1½ pints weak vegetable stock
280ml / ½ pint milk
2 tbs frozen peas
seasoning as required

Pull the lovage leaves off the stalks. You need enough to loosely fill a 560ml / 1 pint jug. If you want to garnish, keep 8 nice ones separate and finely chop the rest. Fry the onions gently in the butter until soft. Add the garlic and fry a few more minutes. Add the potato and stock and cook until the potato is soft. Add the milk and peas and return to the boil. Blend. Add the chopped lovage and blend again. Reheat to just bring back to the boil and serve immediately, topped with the lovage leaves.

Celery and Artichoke Soup

I used to make this for my parents and we still use the same recipe. My dad used to grow Jerusalem artichokes and it seemed natural to grow them at Doune. They grow well here and are a great vegetable to harvest through the winter. We freeze the excess ready for the summer and make this lovely light soup with the bounty. If you don't grow your own, Jerusalem artichokes are now available in some supermarkets and box schemes. The flavour of Jerusalem artichokes is unlike any other and it combines beautifully with the savoury celery to make a really unusual soup.

serves 6

5 to 6 good fresh sticks of celery, washed
6 small pieces of peeled potato (walnut sized)
3 to 4 large Jerusalem artichokes, peeled
1 large onion
25g / 1oz butter
vegetable stock
6 tsp fresh double cream for garnish

Roughly chop the vegetables and fry gently in the butter. Cover well with stock and simmer until soft. Blend until smooth and adjust for seasoning. You may need to add a little more stock to get the thickness you like. Garnish with a swirl of cream.

Scotch Broth

Scotch Broth is not really an exact science, and ours is probably a bit idiosyncratic, but I have tried to give an idea of quantities. Because it is too easy to make it thick and heavy, I prefer not to cook the barley etc. in the soup, but to add it later. (You can freeze what you don't use for another day.) Also, even if you rinse it first it often produces a deposit that I would rather not serve in my soup! If you use 'broth mix' you will have to cook it longer to soften the haricot beans.

serves 8

850ml / 1½ pints strong venison or lamb stock
1 or 2 onions
1 or 2 carrots
¼ medium swede
2 sticks celery
1 small parsnip
Fresh rosemary and thyme, chopped
Salt and pepper
8oz / 225g mixed pearl barley, split green peas and Puy or brown lentils
1 tbs / 15ml tomato purée
½ tin baked beans
dash dry sherry
dash balsamic vinegar
fresh chopped parsley for garnish

Chop the vegetables into fine dice and boil up in the stock with the herbs and seasoning. Rinse the barley, split peas and lentils in a sieve and bring to the boil in water, skim and boil until soft. Drain and rinse until clean, the grains should stay separate. Add as much barley mix to the soup as you like and add the rest of the flavourings to taste. Finish with fresh parsley.

Carrot, Ginger and Honey Soup

This is one of Penny's recipes. It seems a lot of work to grate the carrots but it really does make a difference to the finished soup. The flavours are delicate and finely balanced so don't overdo the ginger or it will overpower the honey.

serves 8

25g / 1oz butter
2 onions, thinly sliced
2cm / 1 inch fresh ginger, peeled, crushed and chopped
725g / 1lb 10oz carrots, peeled and grated
2 tbs clear honey
1 tbs lemon juice
1 tsp salt
freshly ground black pepper
fresh double cream for garnish

Melt the butter and fry the onion and ginger gently for 10 minutes. Add the carrots, honey, lemon juice and salt. Pour in 1.42 litres / 2½ pints of water and simmer for 45 minutes. Grind in plenty of fresh black pepper and liquidise until smooth and creamy adding more water if needed. Garnish with a swirl of cream.

Spiced Cumberland Soup

Toppi, who cooked with us for a couple of years when Ewan was born, brought us this unusual recipe and it's a real favourite. It has such richness and depth that it is hard to believe that it is truly vegetarian. I love to go in the dining room and listen to everyone trying to guess what is in it!

serves 8
2 medium onions
4 medium carrots
40g / 1½ oz butter
8 mushrooms
1 tin tomatoes
560ml / 1 pint vegetable stock
¼ bottle red wine
1 tsp ground allspice
140ml / ¼ pint orange juice
1 tbs redcurrant jelly
½ measure port
salt and pepper
for vegetable stock:
2.28 litres / 4 pints water, 4 garlic cloves, 2 leeks, 2 carrots, 4 stalks thyme, 2 onions, 3 celery stalks, 1 star anise, 2 tsp coriander seeds, ½ tsp peppercorns, 2 bay leaves, ½ to 1 tsp salt.

Simmer the stock for 10 minutes, cool, strain, and use as needed. Or a cube is fine. Roughly chop the onions and carrots and fry in the butter until the onions are soft. Add the mushrooms and cook for a minute more. Add the stock and simmer for 20 minutes or until the carrots are soft. Add the tomatoes and liquidise. Add the rest, taste and adjust the seasoning if needed.

French Onion Soup

This is not a true French onion soup which is meant to be a meal in itself. To allow for more courses we make it lighter with less onion and a smaller croûton. Gruyère cheese is traditional but you can use any you like, we choose a mature Cheddar. The most important things for either version are a really good stock and well caramelised onions.

serves 6
450g / 1lb onions, thinly sliced
25g / 1oz butter
1 tbs Balsamic vinegar
1 glug dry sherry
1.14 litres / 2 pints strong venison or beef stock
salt and freshly ground black pepper
for the croutons: **quality bread, grated cheese, chopped parsley**

Melt the butter in a wide, heavy-based pan and fry the onions until they are an even golden brown. A wide pan ensures maximum contact of the onions with the pan surface and a thick base reduces the chances of burning. The process can take up to an hour but you can speed it up a bit by starting off on a higher heat in which case you must watch and stir to avoid burning, then turn down and sweat gently until very soft. Another tip is to add a teaspoon (no more) of sugar. Add the sherry and vinegar and boil off the alcohol before adding the stock. Boil for a few minutes then taste and season. Melt the cheese on the croutons and place on top.

Cauliflower and Coconut Soup

There is a fair amount of work involved in this soup but it is well worth the effort with great depth of flavour and stunning looks. The strength of the chillies makes a big difference. It is delicious both mild or hot but you may want to adjust for your taste. You can substitute lemon and lime zest for the lemongrass and lime leaves. Also, lemon verbena has a very similar flavour to lemongrass and makes a great substitute.

serves 4

1 can (385g) coconut milk
430ml / ¾ pint vegetable stock
2 cloves garlic, bashed and chopped
2cm / 1 inch piece (thick) fresh ginger, chopped
2 lemongrass sticks, roughly chopped
2 kaffir lime leaves, shredded
1 to 2 whole green chillies, de-seeded and chopped
1 medium onion, thinly sliced
1 tbs coconut oil
1 tsp turmeric
1 tsp sugar
225g / 8oz cauliflower cut into very small florets
1 tbs lime juice
1 tbs soy sauce
1 tsp sesame oil
2 spring onions, shredded into thin 1 inch strips
2 tbs freshly chopped coriander leaf

Heat the first seven ingredients together and simmer for 15 minutes. Leave to infuse for 1 hour or until ready to finish the soup. Fry the onion, turmeric and sugar gently in the oil for 5 minutes. Add the cauliflower florets and stir until they have taken on the golden colour of the turmeric. Strain the coconut stock onto the vegetables and add the lime juice, soy and sesame oil. Simmer gently for 5 minutes. Check the seasoning and immediately before serving, add the spring onion and coriander.

Beetroot and Tomato Soup

You can make this soup with stored beetroot at any time but it is at its best if you use new season beets from August through to November. They are juicier and fresher tasting and the colour is amazing. The other tip for maintaining colour and flavour is to avoid overcooking, so stick to the timing stated. Grating the beets reduces the cooking time and although it seems like a fiddle, it is important. If you are making the soup ahead, cool it quickly by immersing the pan in a sink of cold water and only reheat just before serving. If you don't have chives, finely chopped spring onion leaves are good.

serves 6:
25g / 1oz butter
1 onion, chopped
1 clove garlic, crushed
350g / 12oz fresh beetroot, peeled and grated
1 level tsp ground cumin
½ level tsp ground cinnamon
1 tin chopped tomatoes
1 tbs tomato purée
850ml / 1½ pints vegetable stock
1 tbs soy sauce
salt and pepper to taste
6 tsp sour cream and fresh chives to serve

Melt the butter and fry the onion and garlic gently for 5 minutes to start to soften. Add the beetroot, stir, cover and cook gently for 10 minutes. Add the spices, tomatoes, purée and stock and simmer for 15 minutes until the beetroot is tender. Add the soy and season. Purée and reheat to serve. Mix the sour cream with some snipped chives and a pinch of salt, put a dollop on each bowl of soup and sprinkle with a few more chives.

Doune Crab Soup

When Alan and Mary first came to Doune they put a pot in the bay and enjoyed fresh crab all through the summer. When they started having guests in the house, It was the obvious thing to serve crab and their friend Lawrie gave them this recipe. If you use ready dressed crab meat and don't have the shells for making stock, fish or vegetable stock will do but is obviously not as richly crabby.

serves 6
1 onion
2 cloves garlic, crushed
1 red pepper
2 sticks celery
25g / 1oz butter
25g / 1oz plain flour
850ml / 1½ pints good fish or crab stock
1 small bay leaf
dash of dry sherry
1 tsp anchovy essence
Salt and pepper to taste
6 portions of crab meat, brown and white, the more the better
Lots of fresh chopped lovage and parsley

Make sure the brown crab meat has been blended smooth. Chunky pieces of white meat are good. Finely chop the onion, pepper and celery and gently sauté with the garlic in the butter until soft but not brown. Stir in the flour and cook for a minute or so. Add the stock and bay leaf, and stir through the boil. Simmer for fifteen minutes and remove the bay leaf. Add the other flavourings and the brown crab meat and return to the boil making sure the brown meat is well distributed through the soup. Add the white meat and bring carefully back to simmer then turn off the heat so it does not cook any more. Taste and season as required. Add the fresh herbs and serve immediately.

Crab stock

25g / 1 oz butter
1 onion, chopped
1 clove of garlic, chopped
1 carrot
1 stick celery
4 picked crab shells, bodies and claws (avoid the stomach, filter fingers and legs)
1 slice lemon
1 bay leaf
1 sprig fresh thyme or 1 pinch dried
1 pinch paprika

Gently fry the vegetables in the butter. Add the crab shells and bash to break up. Add the rest plus water to cover. Simmer for half an hour. Strain through a fine sieve or muslin.

Lamb, Leek and Potato Soup

I am bereft in the middle of the summer when leeks are often shot and woody and no good for anything, as this is my favourite soup to use the fabulous lamb stock that we create every time we serve roast lamb. This is a chunky soup, so, (as long as they are not too coarse), I like to use some of the green leaves of the leeks. If you want a blended soup, I would suggest using just the white part and slightly less potato.

serves 6

2 large leeks, well washed
25g / 1oz lamb dripping
1 small clove of garlic
1 tsp chopped fresh thyme leaves
6 medium pieces potato, cut into cubes
850ml / 1½ pints strong lamb stock
salt and freshly ground black pepper
1 tbs fresh double cream
fresh chopped parsley or thyme to garnish

Slice the leeks into 4 lengthways and chop roughly. Fry gently in the dripping with the garlic and thyme until softened. Add the potato, stock and some seasoning and bring to the boil. Simmer until the potatoes are just done. Add the cream, taste and re-season. Sprinkle with parsley or thyme to serve.

Gazpacho

We plan our menus weekly and try to stick with the plan (mostly!). However, when we get really hot weather, we have been known to change at the last minute to a chilled soup to try to cool everything down a bit, and this one is our favourite. Cold food needs strong flavours and good seasoning as the low temperature dulls the palate, and this really fits the bill. You will need some form of blender or food processor and some ice cubes at the ready.

serves 4 to 5
450g / 1lb ripe tomatoes, cored and skinned
½ standard tin chopped tomatoes
½ cucumber, peeled and chopped
3 spring onions, chopped
2 cloves garlic, crushed
½ large red pepper de-seeded and chopped
½ tbs fresh chopped basil or marjoram
4 tbs good olive oil
1½ tbs white wine vinegar
280ml / ½ pint cold water
salt and freshly ground black pepper
for the garnish:
a very small amount of red pepper, cucumber, spring onion, hard boiled egg, and fresh parsley all very finely chopped and mixed together.

Prepare all the ingredients and blend together until smooth. Taste and add more garlic, basil or salt and pepper if needed. Taste again before serving in case the flavour has been dulled by the cold. Serve well chilled with an ice cube and a teaspoon of garnish mix on each bowl.

Courgette and Lemon Soup

I made this soup when I was working as cook for a family one summer holiday. It is light and fresh, but don't be tempted to use old or over large courgettes or the flavour will be bitter. I have given weights for the vegetables as it can be hard to get the balance right.

serves 6
175g / 6oz onions, chopped
25g / 1oz butter
250g / 9oz potatoes, peeled and chopped
zest 1 lemon
990ml / 1¾ pints of half strength vegetable stock
560g / 1¼ lb courgettes, rough chopped
seasoning to taste
juice ½ to 1 lemon

Fry the onion in butter until soft. Add the potatoes, lemon zest, and vegetable stock and simmer until the potatoes are soft. Add the courgettes and simmer for 5 minutes only. Liquidise, taste and season. Do not boil too long on reheating as it will lose the fresh taste. Add enough lemon juice to give it a sharpness to your taste. It needs no garnish as there should be bright green flecks from the courgette skins.

Variation:

Courgette and Basil Soup

I have tried various soups with basil but this idea of using basil pesto is the lightest, tastiest and simplest yet. Jane grows fantastic basil in the greenhouse on the side of her house so we always have our own pesto available to go with the summer glut of courgettes. Use the courgette and lemon soup recipe, omit the lemon zest and juice and add a couple of spoons of pesto to your taste.

Carrot and Orange Soup

This is a lovely easy soup which is great as a vegetarian option. Vegetable stock overpowers the delicate flavour; plain water is best.

serves 8

50g / 2oz butter
2 onions
6 - 8 carrots
2 small potatoes
zest and juice 1 orange
water
salt and freshly ground black pepper
fresh double cream for garnish

Chop the carrots, onions and potatoes and fry gently in the butter for about 5 minutes. Add the zest and water to cover the vegetables. Simmer until the carrots are just done. Liquidise and season to taste. Adjust the consistency with more water if required. Reheat, and just before serving, add the freshly squeezed orange juice. Garnish with a swirl of cream.

Butternut Squash and Coconut Soup

This method of roasting vegetables as a base for a soup gives a really rich result. Sweet potato soup is very good done this way as are carrots and parsnips.

serves 6

450g / 1 lb butternut squash, in chunks
2 tbs coconut oil, melted
1 large onion, cut into 8
1 red pepper, deseeded and cut into 8
1 fresh chilli, deseeded
1 clove garlic, peeled and squashed
1 tsp curry powder
1 (385g) can coconut milk
560ml / 1 pint water
seasoning
toasted coconut to garnish

Preheat the oven to 200°C / gas mark 6. Mix the butternut in the oil with plenty of seasoning and roast for 10 minutes. Reduce to 180°C / gas mark 4 and add the onion, pepper and chilli, giving it all a good mix. Roast for about 20 minutes. Add the garlic and roast a further 5 to 10 minutes. Everything should be really soft. Add the curry powder and roast a couple more minutes. Turn everything, including any stuck on bits, into a pan, add the coconut milk and water and boil for 2 minutes. Blend, and add more water to make your desired consistency. Season to taste, reheat and serve hot with a sprinkle of toasted coconut.

. Cullen Skink

This traditional fish soup from North East Scotland is usually made using milk and cream but we find this version with stock and just a little cream is lighter at the start of a 3-course meal. While using a mixture of vegetable and chicken stock makes a nice soup, for the real deal we would recommend making your own strong fish stock. Start with plenty of fresh fish bones and use water to just cover. Add half an onion, 1 carrot, a stick of celery, a couple of bay leaves and a few black peppercorns, (no salt). Bring to the boil, skim off any scum and simmer gently for half an hour. Cool and strain. Cullen Skink is Jane's favourite soup.

serves 6
2 medium onions, roughly chopped
6 pieces potato, about the size of a mandarin orange, peeled and roughly chopped
2 cloves garlic, crushed
40g / 1½ oz butter
850ml / 1 ½ pints good fish stock (or half in half vegetable and chicken stock)
350g / 12oz smoked haddock fillets, skinned, checked for bones and roughly chopped
freshly ground black pepper (salt only if needed)
freshly grated nutmeg
pinch saffron
110g / 4oz fresh haddock fillets, skinned, checked for bones and roughly chopped
1½ tbs fresh double cream
fresh chopped lovage and parsley

Gently fry the onions and garlic in the butter until the onions are very soft. Add the potatoes and stock and boil until the potatoes are just done. Add the smoked haddock and return to simmering point. Add the seasoning, nutmeg and saffron and taste, saltiness will depend on the smoked fish so go carefully when adding seasoning. Add the fresh haddock and return to simmering point then immediately turn off the heat. Add the cream, a generous amount of herbs, and serve.

Spiced Cullen Skink

Recommended to us by a guest, this lovely soup is our version of a recipe from Glasgow's Mother India restaurant. It is spicy and warming with a great balance of flavours. Chicken stock gives a rich soup; fish stock is lighter.

serves 6

2 medium new potatoes, diced quite small
1 tsp cumin seeds
½ tsp fenugreek seeds
450g / 1lb smoked haddock
2 bay leaves
few gratings nutmeg
1 handful flat leaf parsley, stalks and leaves separated
560ml / 1 pint milk
1 large onion, diced
25g butter / 1oz butter
2 cloves garlic, crushed
1 green chilli, finely chopped
430ml / ¾ pint homemade, unsalted, chicken or fish stock (or water)
½ tsp black pepper
2 tbs double cream
chopped chives

Toss the cumin and fenugreek seeds in a dry pan over a moderate heat until they become fragrant, cool and grind. Put the haddock, bay leaves, nutmeg and parsley stalks in a pan with the milk and poach gently until the fish is cooked. Remove the fish and flake it carefully. Strain the milk and keep it for later. Fry the onion in the butter until starting to soften, add the garlic, chilli and spices and cook gently for a few minutes. Add the potatoes, reserved milk, and stock, and simmer until the potatoes are fully cooked. Add the fish and bring back to the boil. Turn off the heat, add the roughly chopped parsley leaves, pepper and cream, and serve sprinkled with chives.

Main Courses

We balance our menus so that our guests get a full variety of meats and fish through their stay. Likewise, the flavourings and textures; a tomato based casserole one day, light, herb flavoured fish another and chicken in a rich creamy sauce the next. After 25 years we have plenty of recipes to choose from.

fish

Salmon Tagliatelle with Lemon and Basil

Salmon is very good when teamed with strong flavours that would overpower more delicate fish. This seems like a lot of lemon but it really does work. We make our own tagliatelle, which comes up a wonderful golden colour with our vibrant Doune eggs, but bought pasta will do fine!

serves 6
juice 3 lemons
extra virgin olive oil to the same volume as the lemon juice
6 portions salmon fillet, skin off
seasoning
350g /12 oz fresh tagliatelle
freshly grated Parmesan cheese
freshly ground black pepper
1 big handful fresh basil leaves
6 lemon wedges to serve

Preheat the oven to 180°C / gas mark 4. Whisk the lemon juice and olive oil together until well emulsified. Place the salmon pieces on a baking tray and season well. Drizzle a little of the oil and lemon mixture over the fish (use about a quarter of the volume in total). Cover the tray with foil and bake, for 20 minutes or until the fish is no longer translucent but still moist. Bring a very large pan of water to a rolling boil and add a teaspoon of salt and a slug of olive oil. About 5 minutes before the fish is due to be ready, put the rest of the lemon and oil mixture to warm gently in a small pan (it may need re emulsifying first). Add the tagliatelle to the boiling water and swirl it around gently to keep the strands from sticking. Keep on high heat and once it returns to the boil cook for about 3 minutes until al dente. At this stage tear up the basil leaves. Strain the pasta and mix in a little of the warmed lemony juice, a little Parmesan and some freshly ground black pepper. Pile into a warm serving dish. Sprinkle over some more Parmesan and most of the basil. Place the pieces of salmon on top and drizzle with the rest of the warm juice. Top with more Parmesan, the rest of the basil, and garnish with the lemon wedges.

Coriander Haddock with Carrot Pilaf

It is well worth making the full quantity of coriander paste as it freezes really well and can be used for lots of things from pasta to a spread for a mixed salad sandwich. We use it to top baked tomatoes or fill aubergine rolls as a vegetarian version when serving this dish. The pilaf is just so delicious it makes a great meal on its own!

serves 8
8 fillets of haddock or other white fish
225g / 8oz coriander paste
8 slices of lemon
Seasoning
A few fresh coriander leaves for garnish
for the coriander paste: (makes 20 to 25 portions)
2 tsp whole cumin seeds
2 tsp whole coriander seeds
2 tsp whole fenugreek seeds
12 cloves garlic, peeled
10cm / 4 inches fresh ginger, peeled
1 large onion, peeled
1 block creamed coconut
4 green chillies, deseeded
175g / 6oz fresh coriander, include the stalks
2 tsp ground coriander
for the carrot pilaf:
12oz brown Basmati rice
2 onions, thinly sliced
2 tbs coconut oil
10 cardamom pods (remove pod casings)
2 large bay leaves, crushed
2 tsp cumin seeds
large pinch ground cinnamon
2 level tsp salt
710ml / 1¼ pints water
2 large carrots, grated
juice ½ lemon
1 tbs fresh chopped coriander

To make the paste, cook the whole spices in a dry pan until they start to colour a little and smell roasted. Cool and grind. Blend them with all the other paste ingredients in a food processor until smooth. Spread a good teaspoon of paste onto the skinned side of the fillets and roll up. Secure with a cocktail stick and top with a lemon slice. Place the rolls on a baking sheet, season well and cover with foil. Preheat the oven to 180°C / gas mark 4. Once the pilaf has been cooking for about 10 minutes, put the fish in the oven and bake for 20 to 25 minutes.
To make the pilaf: Finely grind the cardamom, bay and cumin seeds. Fry the onions quickly so they take on colour. Add the spices and cook for a few seconds. Stir in the rice and add the water, salt, and carrot. Bring all to the boil, cover and simmer for 25 to 30 minutes until just soft. Turn off the heat, cover and leave for 10 minutes, stirring once to distribute the heat. To serve, stir in the lemon juice and coriander.

Mixed Fish Kebabs

We use monkfish, salmon, scallops and prawns but any combination of firm-fleshed fish or shellfish is fine. We tend to keep flavourings simple and serve with classic buttery hollandaise and new potatoes but the more spicy variation served with rice is equally good. For large numbers, it is easiest to cook the kebabs in the oven but if you prefer to use a grill or barbecue, make sure it is very hot before you start. Cook, turning 4 times, for about 10 minutes in total or until the fish is cooked through.

serves 4
700g / 1½ lb total mixed fish and shellfish
1 red onion
1 small red pepper
2 small courgettes
½ lemon
25g / 1oz melted butter
juice ½ lemon
sea salt flakes
freshly ground black pepper
fresh chopped flat leaf parsley
for the hollandaise sauce:
1 egg yolk
1 tbs water
85g / 3oz unsalted butter, diced
juice approximately 1 small lemon
salt, pepper and pinch cayenne

If using wooden skewers, soak them in water for 15 minutes. Preheat the oven to 180°C / gas mark 4. Cut the fish into large chunks. Quarter the red onion and pull apart the layers. Deseed the pepper and cut into 8. Cut each courgette into 4 chunks. Cut the ½ lemon into 4. Thread onto 4 skewers, dividing the ingredients equally. Mix the lemon juice into the melted butter and brush the mixture over the kebabs. Sprinkle generously with salt and pepper, place on a baking tray and cook for 20 minutes or until the fish is done. The hollandaise will take about 10 to 15 minutes to make. Put the yolks and water in a small heavy-based pan and whisk to blend. Add the butter and heat gently whisking all the time. Once the butter is melted, turn up the heat to medium and continue whisking until it thickens. Remove from the heat, and add lemon juice and seasoning to taste. Do not leave the sauce unattended while it is being made. It will keep for some time, just cover the pan with a towel, but do not attempt to reheat it. Drizzle the sauce over the cooked kebabs and sprinkle with parsley.

To make the sauce into foaming hollandaise:
Whisk an egg white until it is very stiff and fold into the sauce immediately. This makes the sauce lighter and it goes further.

Variation: **Spicy Fish Kebabs**
In a large bowl, whisk together 2 tbs olive oil, juice ½ a lemon, 1 crushed garlic clove, 1 tsp chilli flakes, 1 tsp ground cumin, 1 dsp chopped fresh marjoram or coriander, salt flakes, freshly ground black pepper and a pinch of saffron. Add the fish and vegetables and mix thoroughly. Leave in the fridge to marinade for about 30 minutes. Thread on skewers and cook as above. Sprinkle with more of your chosen fresh herb.

Baked Salmon with Scallop Sauce

Although we have lots of lovely salmon recipes we keep coming back to this one. It is hugely popular, simply cooked salmon done to perfection and a rich yet sharp sauce using fabulous local scallops, what could be better? When we started we used to cook a whole salmon and serve it from the bone in the Dining Room, we have found ready portioned fillets so much less stressful!

serves 6
6 portions fresh salmon fillet
25g / 1oz butter
seasoning
white wine vinegar
lemon and dill to garnish
for the scallop sauce:
6 scallops
40g / 1½ oz butter
1 clove garlic
25g / 1oz flour
200ml / 7 fl oz milk
85ml / 3 fl oz dry white wine
1 tbs lemon juice, or more to taste
1 tsp anchovy essence
25g / 1 oz strong Cheddar cheese
seasoning to taste
½ tsp fresh chopped dill

Preheat the oven to 180°C / gas mark 4. Lay the salmon pieces on a baking tray and top each with a knob of butter and plenty of seasoning. Splash a little wine vinegar into the tray and cover with foil. Bake for 20 minutes or until the fish is just done.

Cut the scallops up into small chunks. Fry with the garlic in half the butter for one minute only. Drain and remove. Add the rest of the butter and make a roux with the flour. Cook gently for a minute or so, add the milk and whisk until boiling and thickened. Add the other ingredients, bring back to the boil and season to taste. Just before serving, return the scallops and heat through gently. Do not boil or the scallops will overcook and toughen. Add the chopped dill and serve with the fish.

Baked Fish with Fennel and Tomatoes

I have no idea what the programme was but I saw this on television while on holiday and once it had finished I suddenly realised that it would be a great one for the Dining Room. We then had a panic to find pen and paper and try to remember what was in it. Right or wrong it works really well and I love it. Sautéing and then baking the fennel gives it a mellow, nutty flavour which blends beautifully with the other ingredients. We usually use haddock but it would work with any white fish.

serves 6
1 large bulb fennel
25g / 1 oz butter
½ tsp whole fennel seeds
½ tsp whole cumin seeds
3 large tomatoes, roughly chopped
1 tsp sugar
¼ tsp salt

freshly ground black pepper
750g / 1lb 14oz white fish fillets, cut into large chunks
175g / 6oz Feta cheese, cut into small cubes
50g / 2oz butter
juice 1 lemon
1 tbs fresh chopped parsley
1 dsp fresh chopped fennel fronds or herb

Turn the oven on to 190°C / gas mark 5. Remove and discard any very hard core and tough stalks from the fennel. Keep any green fronds for the garnish and slice the bulb. Fry gently in the 25g / 1oz of butter until starting to soften. Add the seeds and fry for 1 minute. Add the tomatoes and seasoning and bring to the boil. Cook for a minute until the tomatoes are just starting to soften and pour into a low sided ovenproof dish. Place the chunks of fish on top and sprinkle with the cheese. Bake, uncovered, in the preheated oven for 15 to 20 minutes until the fish is just cooked. When nearly done melt the rest of the butter, add the lemon juice, bubble and pour evenly over the dish. Top with the chopped herbs

Ascot Salmon

Jane named this dish because she says the garnish of a lemon twist and herb leaf on top of the pesto looks like a fancy hat. When we serve it together it always makes us smile. We have tried lots of different pestos (see below, use the same proportions of nuts and herbs) depending on the season, and they all work really well with salmon which marries happily with strong flavours. I choose not to use pine nuts because they don't keep for long and are too expensive to throw out. Other nuts work just as well.

serves 6
6 portions fresh salmon fillet
olive oil
seasoning
white wine vinegar
6 lemon slices and mint leaves to garnish
for Hazelnut and Mint Pesto:
25g / 1oz hazelnuts, toasted and skinned
50g / 2oz fresh tender mint leaves (not peppermint)
1 clove garlic
25g / 1oz grated Parmesan cheese
salt and pepper
juice 1 lemon
2 tbs good olive oil

Preheat the oven to 180°C / gas mark 4. Lay the salmon pieces on a baking tray. Brush with olive oil and season well. Splash a little wine vinegar into the tray. Cover with foil and bake for 20 minutes.
Blend all the pesto ingredients together adding a little more olive oil if needed to make a soft paste. Place a dollop of pesto on each piece of fish and garnish with lemon and mint.
other pestos:
Basil and cashew
Rocket and walnut
Flat leaf parsley and almond

Salmon Filo Parcels

We are always on the lookout for new ideas for serving salmon and using apples was a thought bubbling under for years. The combination using hot smoked salmon was a sudden inspiration, and when we tried it we knew we had a winner! Making the individual parcels is a bit of a fiddle but they do look fantastic. If you don't want to spend the time, you can always make a pie with the filo scrunched on top.

serves 6

2 large cooking apples, peeled and cored
a little sugar
juice ½ lemon
2 portions fresh salmon fillet
salt and pepper
2 portions hot smoked salmon
4½ sheets filo pastry
melted butter for brushing

Cook the apples gently with a splash of water until pulpy and mash them up. Add sugar to just bring out the apple flavour, but not sweeten it, and then add the lemon juice. Leave to cool. Cook the fresh salmon fillet by poaching gently in water with seasoning and a dash of vinegar. Drain and leave to cool. Skin and flake both types of fish carefully and gently fold into the apple purée keeping whole flakes of fish as much as possible. Preheat the oven to 200°C / gas mark 6. To make the parcels, cut the filo sheets into 8. Brush 4 of the cut pieces lightly with butter and layer up, offsetting so that the points of the squares form a star shape. Brush 2 more pieces, lay on top of one another and place a tablespoon of filling in the middle, fold up to make a parcel. Place the parcel, folded side down, in the centre of the star. Scrunch up the rest of the filo to make a bag around the parcel. Place on a buttered baking sheet and touch up with more butter as needed. Repeat to make 5 more parcels. Bake for 5 to 10 minutes until the pastry is light brown and then cover lightly with foil and cook 10 more minutes until fully crisp and the filling is hot.

Haddock with Parmesan Crust

This has been one of our favourite recipes for many years. We try hard to source sustainable fish and rely on information from our supplier Andy Race in Mallaig. The haddock comes from different fisheries during the season depending on when the fish are not spawning. When we can't get suitable haddock we use hake or saithe. For us, it doesn't seem right to serve this without dauphinoise potatoes, (see page 70), although I'm sure it would be great with anything.

serves 4

4 large fillets haddock
60g / 2½ oz grated Parmesan
85g / 3oz wholemeal breadcrumbs
generous handful fresh chopped parsley
freshly ground black pepper
60g / 2½ oz unsalted butter, melted
parsley and lemon wedges to garnish

Preheat the oven to 230°C / gas mark 8. Mix the Parmesan, crumbs, and parsley and season with plenty of pepper. (No salt needed as Parmesan is quite salty already.) Stir in the melted butter to make a crumbly mixture. Place the fillets on a metal tray and top with the crumb mixture. When ready to cook, make sure the oven is up to temperature and bake on the top shelf for about 7 minutes. The crust should be brown and the fish just starting to think about yielding a bit of juice.

Variation: Aubergine Layer

For a vegetarian version, roast half an aubergine cut into two thick slices (cut length-wise) and half a red pepper (cut into 4) until soft. Layer with some slices of fresh tomato using the aubergine top and bottom. Make the crumbs using a vegetarian cheese and spread on top. Cook as for the fish.

Salmon with Bacon

The sharpness of the cornichon and capers is a great way to cut the richness of salmon.

serves 6

3 spring onions, finely chopped
6 cornichon, finely chopped
24 capers, finely chopped
1 tbs chopped fresh dill
freshly ground black pepper
6 tsp mayonnaise
6 rashers thinly sliced smoked bacon
6 portions salmon fillet, skin off

Preheat the oven to 200°C / gas mark 6. Mix the spring onion, gherkin, capers. dill and black pepper into the mayonnaise. If the bacon is at all thick, stretch it slightly by laying on a board and 'spreading' it with a blunt knife. Place the mayonnaise mixture on top of the salmon fillets and wrap with the bacon, join underneath. Bake (without covering) for 15 minutes. The bacon should be crispy and the salmon will be done and still moist inside.

Prawn buffet salads

Prawn night is something of a Doune tradition, a huge mound of fresh, local langoustine served buffet style - it can be a long evening! We started catching our own but once we got busier we had to source from local boats and we still often use our original supplier. To accompany, we prepare a big array of salads with different flavours, textures and colours. We have collected many over the years and this is a selection of our favourites. All salads serve approximately 6 depending on what else you are serving.

Garlicky Rice Salad

Our favourite rice salad. The dressing works well for a cheat Caesar Salad.

1 crisp red apple, cored and roughly chopped
juice ½ lemon
3 tbs white rice, cooked and cooled
2 sticks celery, roughly chopped

for the seed mix

1 dsp pumpkin seeds
1 dsp sunflower seeds
1 dsp cashew nuts
1 dsp flaked almonds
1 tsp olive oil
sea salt flakes

For the dressing:

3 dsp mayonnaise
1 clove garlic, crushed
1 tsp anchovy essence
1 tbs Worcestershire Sauce
juice ½ lemon
water as needed

Gently cook the nuts and seeds in the olive oil until starting to brown and pop and sprinkle with salt.
To make the dressing, shake everything together in a jar; it should be like double cream so add a little water if it is too thick. Chop the apple, mix with the lemon juice and add the rice and celery. Mix in ¾ of the seed mix and the dressing. Sprinkle with the remaining seeds.

Red Salad

This is one of our most asked for recipes. It looks and tastes stunning when made fresh but it really doesn't keep well so do leave dressing it until the very last moment before serving.

1 apple, skin on, cored and diced
¼ red cabbage, very finely sliced
2 carrots, grated
½ red pepper, thinly sliced
½ green pepper, thinly sliced
½ yellow pepper, thinly sliced
1 mango, in chunks

for the dressing:

2 tbs white wine vinegar
4 tbs light olive oil
1 tbs sugar
1 tsp garam masala
½ tsp ground cumin
½ tsp ground turmeric

Mix all the prepared vegetables together. Whisk the dressing ingredients together. You may not need all the dressing, as the quantity of salad varies a surprising amount depending on the size of the vegetables. I suggest using about half the dressing first and see how it goes, you don't want to drown it.

Carrot and Cucumber Salad

The sweet chilli dressing is particularly popular in the Dining Room. This salad goes well with our carrot hummus on page 24.

1 red chilli, finely chopped
½ cup sugar
½ cup wine vinegar
1 green chilli, finely chopped
½ large cucumber
2 carrots
½ medium red onion

Boil the vinegar, sugar and red chilli in a non-reactive pan for about 5 minutes until starting to get syrupy. Cool, then add the green chilli. Cut the cucumber in half lengthwise and then into chunky slices. Peel the carrots and make long strips with the peeler. Peel and very thinly slice the onion. Mix the prepared vegetables together in a large bowl, pour over the dressing and toss well.

Beetroot and Raspberry Salad

This was inspired by a rather strange but oddly delicious dish, produced by my aunt years ago, of beetroot set in a raspberry jelly! We source fantastic intensely fruity raspberry vinegar and top quality walnut oil and this interesting flavour combination becomes something very special. This goes particularly well with our Onion Tart on page 19.

1 soft lettuce
350g / 12oz cooked beetroot
2 tbs walnut pieces
2 tbs fresh raspberries, optional
1 tbs raspberry vinegar
1 tbs walnut oil

Lay sliced beets on a bed of the lettuce and sprinkle on the walnuts and raspberries. Whisk together the oil and vinegar and pour on at the last minute.

meat

Red, Spiced, Slow Cooked Lamb

This was one of Penny's recipes. The original was for lamb shanks which are delicious, but, since we buy whole lamb carcasses, we don't have enough shanks to serve everyone, so we adapted it to use diced shoulder. If you use shanks you will need 8 and you may like to cook it even longer.

serves 8

1.125 kg / 2½ lb stewing lamb in chunks
salt and freshly ground black pepper
1½ tsp coriander seeds, lightly crushed
1½ tsp dried rosemary
1½ tsp dried oregano
2 tbs plain flour
1 tbs olive oil
2 cloves garlic, peeled and crushed
2 carrots, diced
3 sticks celery, diced
2 large onions, finely diced
1 large or 2 small fresh red chillies
3 tbs balsamic vinegar
280ml / ½ pint dry white wine
1 tin (50g) anchovy fillets
1 tin chopped tomatoes (2 if using shanks)
1 handful roughly chopped fresh basil
1 handful roughly chopped flat leaf parsley

Preheat the oven to 150°C / gas mark 2. Toss the lamb in the seasoning, coriander seeds, herbs and flour. Brown the meat in the oil quickly and remove to a casserole dish. In the same frying pan, sweat the garlic, vegetables and chilli until the onions are softened. Add the balsamic vinegar and boil. Add this to the casserole with the white wine, anchovies and tomatoes. Cover and cook in the oven for 4 hours until tender. Just before serving, add the fresh herbs.

Variation: Red Spiced Pork

Shoulder pork can be used and only takes 2 hours to cook. The heat of the chilli comes through more as does the flavour of the fresh herbs.

Venison and Blackcurrant Casserole

I am always trying out ways to use our garden produce and I was really happy with this unusual combination. The flavours of both blackcurrant and artichoke come through really well. You do need the sugar, or else the blackcurrants make it too sharp.

serves 8

6 tbs olive oil
3 to 4 onions
1 dsp sugar
1.35kg / 3lb diced venison
2 heaped tbs flour
¾ bottle red wine
350g / 12 oz blackcurrants
350g / 12 oz peeled Jerusalem artichokes, roughly chopped
salt and pepper to taste

Preheat the oven to 150°C / gas mark 2. Peel the onions keeping the root end intact and cut into 4 or 6 depending on size. Fry in half the oil at a reasonably high heat so that they start to caramelise. Add the sugar and continue to brown, stirring often to avoid burning. Remove to a casserole. Fry the venison, in batches, in the rest of the oil and add to the onions. Add the flour to the casserole and stir it in. Deglaze the pan with some of the red wine, add the rest and bring to the boil. Add this, the artichokes, blackcurrants and seasoning to the casserole. Mix well and, stirring continuously, bring to a simmer. Cook in the oven for 3 to 4 hours until tender.

Pork in Sloe Gin

When our guests ask for a recipe we are always happy to oblige but we ask for one of their favourite recipes in return. This was one of the very first swaps, not exactly as the original but the idea was there, and it has been a regular in the Dining Room ever since. It is Martin's favourite pork recipe. Chilean Flame raisins are large and black, and plump up on cooking to look like sloes although they are there for flavour, not just for show. While making the dish smoother the cream does take an edge off the flavour; the choice is yours.

serves 8

1.6 kg / 3½ lb diced pork
25g / 1oz butter
1 tbs olive oil
175ml / 6 fl oz sloe gin
350ml / 12 fl oz vegetable stock
small handful raisins (Chilean Flame if possible)
1 dsp cornflour mixed with a little water
1 tbs double cream (optional)

Preheat the oven to 150°C / gas mark 2. Fry the pork briefly in the butter and oil, drain and put in a casserole dish. Add the raisins, sloe gin and stock; the liquid should just cover the meat. Bring slowly to a very gentle simmer and transfer to cook in the oven for 2 hours. When done, thicken the liquid with the cornflour, and add the cream if liked.

Venison Tagine with Orange Couscous

This is one of Penny's recipes and it is spectacular. The combination with the orange flavoured couscous is perfect. We make it as an oven casserole instead of a classic top cooked tagine. It also works really well with lamb.

serves 6

2 onions, sliced
4 cloves of garlic, sliced
2cm / 1 inch piece ginger, grated
1 tbs mild olive oil
½ tsp ground cinnamon
½ tsp ground allspice
½ tsp ground cumin
½ tsp ground turmeric
1 tsp ground coriander
1 tsp cracked black pepper
1 tsp paprika
1 tsp salt
1 tin chopped tomatoes
280ml ½ pint water
85g / 3oz apricots, halved
85g / 3oz prunes, halved
zest and juice 1 large orange
2 star anise
1kg / 2¼ lb diced venison
1 tbs mild olive oil
½ tbs honey

for the couscous:

300g / 10 ½ oz couscous
1 red onion, finely sliced
zest and juice 1 large orange
1 tbs olive oil
1 tsp salt
2 tbs fresh chopped parsley

Preheat the oven to 150°C / gas mark 2. Put the red onion and orange zest for the couscous in a bowl, pour on the juice, cover and leave. In a large flameproof casserole dish fry the onions, garlic and ginger in the oil until soft. Add the spices and fry gently for a minute more. Add the tomatoes, water, apricots, prunes, zest of the orange and star anise. Fry the meat in a separate pan in the rest of the oil and add to the onion mix. Cook in the oven for 3 to 4 hours until tender. Add the orange juice and honey. When ready to serve, put the couscous into a flat tray with a reasonable lip. Drain the onion and put the juice and zest with the oil and salt into a pan. Add water to make a total of 450ml / 16 fl oz of liquid and bring to the boil. Pour on to the couscous, stir well and cover with another tray. After 5 minutes give it another stir, add the reserved onion and parsley and cover again. After 5 more minutes stir well and serve with the tagine.

Spiced Lamb

This dish came from my days working for British Meat before I was married. It was a really a kebab recipe but at Doune, it works better as a casserole. The marinade starts to tenderise the meat so it doesn't take as long to cook as our other lamb casseroles.

serves 8

1.6kg / 3½ lb lamb, diced
280ml / ½ pint plain yoghurt
2 tsp ground ginger
1 tsp ground cumin
1 tsp ground coriander

2 cloves garlic, crushed
3 tbs lime juice cordial
½ tsp salt
2 tsp cornflour
1 red roasted pepper for garnish

Mix everything except the cornflour together, cover, and marinate in the fridge for at least 3 hrs.
Preheat the oven to 170°C / gas mark 3. Transfer to a casserole dish, bring to a simmer and cook in the oven for 2 to 2½ hours until tender. Thicken the sauce with a little cornflour. Garnish with a swirl of yoghurt and strips of roasted pepper.

Variation: Spiced Meatballs

Mix 900g / 2lb minced lamb with seasoning, garlic, curry powder, mango chutney, breadcrumbs and egg. Use wet hands to form into 32 meatballs. Fry quickly to brown, place on a lined roasting tin, and bake at 180°C / gas mark 4 for 15 to 20 minutes. Place in a serving dish, pour the marinade as above all over, add a lime in thin slices, and return to the oven to bake until bubbling well. Serve with fresh coriander and quinoa with mint, tomatoes, spring onions and lemon.

Pork in Mustard and Cream

Be warned this recipe is very, very rich so a little goes a long way. However, it is very easy to make, extremely delicious and perfect for a special occasion. Simple brown rice or new potatoes and crisp green vegetables in season will balance the richness. I would also avoid a creamy dessert.

serves 4
2 onions, sliced
2 cloves garlic, crushed
25g / 1oz butter
700g / 1½ lb diced pork
seasoned flour
85ml / 3 fl oz hot vegetable stock
85ml / 3 fl oz double cream
1½ tbs grainy mustard

Preheat the oven to 150°C / gas mark 2. Fry the onions and garlic in the butter until soft and transfer to a casserole dish. Coat the meat lightly in flour and fry briefly in the pan, in batches if needed. Add to the casserole. Add the stock, mustard and cream, mix well and bring to a simmer. Cook in the oven for about 2 hours or until the meat is tender.

Roasts

A traditional roast is one of our specialities and is included in every week's menu. For all Venison or Lamb, we start with a very hot, (240°C / gas mark 9) preheated oven with the joint as high up in the oven as it will fit, and roast for 5 to 15 minutes depending on the size. This seals the outside and starts the browning process. Then we add flavourings and slow it right down to 150°C / gas mark 2 on the bottom shelf for the main cooking time. We stop the cooking well before done (if using a probe you are looking for a temperature in the mid 60's centigrade) then let the joint rest (kept warm under foil and lots of towels) and hey presto, lovely moist, tender meat. The rule of thumb for resting is about half as long as the cooking time which allows the meat to continue cooking slowly using its own heat. A big haunch can have 1½ hours resting while a small joint just half an hour.

Our favourite way with **Roast Venison** is to spread a thick honey and mustard paste all over the joint after the hot stage, so making even more of a seal to keep in the juices. To carve we scrape off the mustard mixture and discard it, it is too strong to eat and has done its job keeping the meat from drying out and imparting extra flavour. For the gravy we add some red wine to the meat juices, bubble it hard for a few minutes to drive off the harsh alcohol, then thicken and season to our taste. We are, of course, lucky to be able to source beautiful local venison which we choose not to hang very long, just enough to tenderise and bring on flavour but not to get over gamey. We always serve our home-made rowan jelly and horseradish sauce.

For Rowan Jelly:
1.35kg / 3lb rowan berries (off main stalks)
900g / 2lb apples, washed and chopped
1.14 litres / 2 pints water
2 tbs any red berries
sugar
Simmer the fruit including the berries in the water until well softened. Strain overnight (do not squeeze) and measure the juice which should be about 850ml / 1½ pints. If it is more, reduce it to this. Add sugar at the rate of 450g per 560ml of liquid. (1lb per pint.) Boil to setting point and jar.

For Horseradish Sauce:
1 tbs mayonnaise
1 tsp Dijon mustard
1 tbs white wine vinegar
4 tbs grated horseradish
1 tbs cream, whipped

For **Roast Lamb**, after the initial blast of heat, we pour dry cider over the top, rub the surface of the meat with crushed garlic, and sprinkle with fresh chopped rosemary and salt. This makes a wonderfully flavoured gravy which we skim of fat, season and slightly thicken. The cider is sometimes a little too sharp but a teaspoon of redcurrant jelly will sort that out. We always serve with mint sauce using chopped apple mint fresh from the garden, malt vinegar to just cover and sugar to taste. It is best put together at the very last minute for the freshest taste and the most amazing colour. Traditional roasties and vegetables are great, and I love to do baked tomatoes with garlic butter and fresh rosemary. We also sometimes serve roast lamb with Dauphin potatoes (page 70) or new potatoes and ratatouille.

Roast Pork is slightly different as you have the crackling to consider. For succulence, we sometimes soak pork for a few hours in brine (1 tbs sugar and 1 tbs salt to 225ml / 8 fl oz water) but we make sure the skin is not under the liquid. For good crackling the skin must be really dry, we pat it well with kitchen paper and rub on some olive oil and a good sprinkling of salt. To start with, the oven should be preheated to 220°C / gas mark 7 which is hot enough to get the crackling started but not so hot that it burns. We cook at this for 20 to 30 minutes by which time the crackling should be well blistered. We then reduce the heat to 180°C / gas mark 4 until cooked. Pork is dense and takes longer than other meats to cook through. It should be cooked to 75° centigrade. Crackling should not be covered or it will go soft, so we rest for just 20 to 30 minutes in a warm place. If all the skin is not crackled you can pop it under a hot grill just before serving but keep a close watch on it or it will burn. Our favourite accompaniment is apples in Calvados.

For Calvados Apples for 6:

2 eating apples
20g / ¾ oz unsalted butter
20g / ¾ oz sugar
1½ tbs Calvados

Peel and core the apples and slice. Fry the slices gently in the butter until starting to soften. Sprinkle over the sugar and cook gently to melt, stirring carefully. Pour in the Calvados and bubble. Cook gently until the apple is coated with a shiny syrup.

Venison Olives

When Mary used to have guests in her house, one of her favourite recipes was beef olives using an unusual lemony stuffing. More recently, in the Dining Room, we have served this version using venison to make the olives.

serves 6

175g / 6 oz fresh white breadcrumbs
1 tbs chopped fresh parsley
zest 1 lemon
seasoning
1 egg, beaten
12 thin slices of venison haunch, beaten flat
1 tbs mild olive oil
25g / 1oz butter
2 to 3 onions, sliced
1 clove garlic, crushed
175g / 6oz mushrooms, sliced
185ml / 6½ fl oz red wine
salt and fresh ground black pepper
2 bay leaves
two small sprigs fresh rosemary

Preheat the oven to 150°C / gas mark 2. Mix the first 5 ingredients to make a stuffing, spread this on the slices of venison, roll up and secure with cocktail sticks. Using some of the of oil and butter, fry the olives quickly to brown them, and place in a baking tin in a single layer. Add a little more fat and fry the onions until turning brown then add the garlic and mushrooms. Fry for a few more minutes and spread over the top of the meat. Deglaze the pan with the red wine and add the herbs and seasoning. Bubble to reduce a little and pour over the meat, it should not come more than halfway up the olives. Cover with foil and cook for 3 to 4 hours in the oven until tender.

Venison Pie

The meat for this pie is the way my mum would have cooked stewing beef and we think its simple flavours are the best to combine with buttery flaky pastry and not overpower it. Using ground white pepper, only a little wine and really long cooking are key. Our puff pastry recipe is on page 160 or if you prefer flaky pastry this is on page 161. Alternatively, use an all butter ready-made pastry.

serves 6

1kg / 2¼ lb stewing venison
1 medium onion, finely chopped
1 tbs plain flour
1 tsp salt
½ tsp ground white pepper
3 tbs red wine
225g / 8oz button mushrooms, halved
25g / 1oz butter
puff pastry made with 175g / 6oz flour or 350g / 12oz bought puff.

Preheat the oven to 150°C / gas mark 2. Put the meat, onions, flour, and seasoning in a large casserole dish and mix well. Add the wine and enough water to just barely cover, and mix again. Bring slowly to simmering point, stirring a few times, cover and cook in the oven for 3 to 4 hours until very tender.

Prepare the pastry to fit your pie dish but put it onto a baking sheet, glaze with a little milk if you want. Increase the oven temperature to 220°C / gas mark 7, remove the casserole and put in the pastry for about 20 minutes. Fry the mushrooms quickly in the butter until starting to brown and add to the meat. Pour into the pie dish and place in the oven on a low shelf under the pastry to keep warm. When the pastry is well puffed and a good brown colour, transfer it to the top of the pie to serve.

Pork in Ale Gravy

This is based on a Tom Kerridge recipe. We settled on pork instead of meatballs and fewer herbs but it still has his characteristic big flavour. Any beer or pale ale will do. The knob of butter prevents the beer from foaming over while boiling.

serves 8

1 onion, sliced
4 cloves garlic, sliced
1 tbs dried rosemary
2 pints beer
85g / 3oz butter
2 onions, sliced
4 tbs plain flour
1 tsp mustard powder
½ tsp dried rosemary
½ tsp dried oregano
½ tsp dried sage
¾ tsp cracked black pepper
1 tsp salt
1.35 kg / 3 lb diced pork
280ml / ½ pint strong chicken stock

Put the one onion, garlic, rosemary, beer and a knob of the butter in a large pan and boil until reduced to a ¼ pint. In half the remaining butter fry the onions quickly until well caramelised and put into a large casserole dish. Preheat the oven to 150°C / gas mark 2. Mix the flour with all the herbs and seasoning. Roll the pork pieces in the flour mixture to lightly coat. Fry the pork in the rest of the butter and add to the onions. Add the stock to the beer and bring to the boil then strain onto the pork and onions. Mix well and bring to simmering point. Cover and cook in the oven for 2 hours or until tender.

Navarin of Lamb

One of my mother's very traditional recipes. Simple but so, so good. If you can get older lamb or hogget, all to the good.

serves 8

1.125 kg / 2½ lb stewing lamb in chunks
1 tbs lamb dripping
3 large carrots in rings
¼ swede in chunks
2 large onions in thin slices
3 tins chopped tomatoes
1 tbs tomato purée
salt and ground white pepper

Preheat the oven to 150°C / gas mark 2. Fry the lamb in the dripping in a heatproof casserole dish. Mix in the other ingredients, bring to a simmer, place in the oven and cook for 3 to 4 hours until very tender

Venison Slices with Port and Redcurrant Sauce

In the days before mobile phones when yachts used to arrive without contacting us hoping for a meal at short notice, we used to keep some quick cooking emergency meat and fish in the freezer and this was one of the recipes we used. Although the recipes we chose were very easy I'm glad we don't have to do the short notice thing any more! The best cuts for this are loin or fillet but any cut suitable for frying will be good.

Serves 2

350g / 12oz tender venison or beef, sliced 1.3cm / ½ in thick
10g / ½ oz butter
½ tbs mild olive oil
1 clove garlic, crushed
110g / 4oz button mushrooms, sliced
4 tbs venison or vegetable stock
2 tsp red wine vinegar
½ glass red wine
1 good glug Port
1 good pinch fresh chopped rosemary
5 Juniper berries, crushed
1 tsp redcurrant jelly
salt and freshly ground black pepper
2 ½ tbs fresh double cream

Get the frying pan very hot and flash fry the meat to your liking in the oil, butter and garlic. Remove to a serving dish and keep warm. Fry the mushrooms until they brown and add to the meat. Put the stock, vinegar, wine, herbs and red currant jelly into the pan, and boil hard to reduce by half. Season and add two tablespoons of the cream. Bubble a little until the sauce thickens slightly. Pour over the meat and mushrooms and drizzle with the rest of the cream.

Chorizo Pork

For this recipe it really makes a difference to go to the trouble of skinning and thinly slicing the chorizo.

serves 8

1.125 kg / 2½ lb diced shoulder pork
225g / 8oz chorizo sausage, skinned and thinly sliced
2 medium red onions, thickly sliced
2 cloves garlic, peeled and crushed
2 tbs olive oil

1 large or 2 small red peppers, sliced and roasted
2 tins tomatoes
1 tbs fresh thyme (or 1 tsp dried)
pinch saffron powder
4 tbs white wine vinegar
280ml / ½ pint white wine
1 small jar pitted black olives
I dsp cornflour
fresh thyme leaves to garnish

Preheat the oven to 150°C / gas mark 2. Fry the pork quickly in half the olive oil and remove to a casserole dish. Sauté the chorizo in the rest of the oil, drain and add to the pork. In this flavoured oil, quickly sauté the onions and garlic. Add to the casserole with all the rest of the ingredients. It is unlikely to require extra seasoning. Bring to a gentle simmer and cook in the oven for 2 hours until the pork is tender. Thicken very slightly with the cornflour and sprinkle with fresh thyme to garnish.

Venison in Skye Black

We have an excellent local brewery on Skye and their dark beer is perfect for this which is my favourite venison recipe.

serves 8
1 tbs olive oil
25g / 1oz butter
225g / 8oz smoked streaky bacon, chopped
3 onions, roughly chopped
4 cloves garlic, crushed
1.35kg / 3lb stewing venison
2 red peppers, roughly chopped
1 tbs plain flour
1 bottle Skye Black or similar
1 tin chopped tomatoes
110g / 4 oz pitted black olives
110g / 4 oz dried prunes, halved
1 tbs chopped fresh rosemary
salt and freshly ground black pepper

Preheat the oven to 150°C / gas mark 2. Fry the bacon in half the oil and butter until crisp, drain and transfer to a casserole dish. In the same frying pan, using the bacon fat, fry the onions and garlic and add to the casserole. Add the rest of the oil and butter to the frying pan and fry the venison (in batches if it is too crowded) to brown it, then add to the casserole. Stir in the rest of the ingredients and bring gently to the simmer. Cook in the oven for 3 to 4 hours until the meat is very tender.

chicken

For any of the chicken recipes here that require stock, I would highly recommend making your own. It will be the making of the dish. Either make a batch with roast chicken carcasses and keep bags in the freezer or cut portions for the recipe off a whole chicken and use the central carcass that is left. Assuming a portion is two small-ish pieces, a small chicken will give 4 good portions, a large can make 6, and you can always make up numbers with some ready cut portions. Cover the bones with cold water, bring to the boil, cover and simmer for about an hour. For strong stock, I reduce the liquid by about a half.

Chicken with Tarragon and Lime

I love using tarragon, it has a fabulous mellow flavour and it grows really well here at Doune so we always have a fresh supply through the summer. If you are buying a plant be sure to get French Tarragon which has the best flavour. Tarragon vinegar is difficult to find in the shops but very easy to make yourself. Simply pick some fresh, clean tarragon leaves and pack into a sterile glass jar. Heat some white wine vinegar to simmering point and pour onto the tarragon. Put on the lid and allow to infuse for a week or so. Keep it cool and it will last all summer; then make a fresh batch for the winter before the herb dies down.

serves 4

4 chicken breasts
1 tbs seasoned flour
25g / 1 oz butter
4 spring onions, finely chopped
2 tbs tarragon vinegar
140ml / ¼ pint dry white wine
2 tbs chopped fresh tarragon
1 lime, grated zest and juice
4 tbs double cream

Coat the chicken in seasoned flour. In a large deep frying pan, fry the chicken in the butter for about 2 minutes each side. Remove and keep warm. Add the spring onions and fry until soft. Add the vinegar, wine and lime juice and reduce until syrupy. Add half the tarragon and half the lime zest, and return the chicken to the pan. Cover and simmer for 15 minutes or so until done, adding just a little water if it gets too dry. Remove to a serving dish and keep warm. Add the cream and bubble for a minute or so, it will thicken slightly. Add the rest of the tarragon and lime, taste and season and pour over the chicken.

Mojo Chicken with Cuban Rice and Beans

This is a zingy and colourful dish. To roast whole cumin seeds toss them in a small pan over a high heat until they smell fantastic and start to take on colour. Once cool they are easy to grind in a bowl with the back of a spoon. The rice is definitely best with homemade chicken stock.

serves 8

8 chicken portions, each cut in 2
1 orange, coarse zest and juice
2 limes, coarse zest and juice
10 large cloves garlic, roughly chopped
1½ tsp salt
2 tsp ground cumin
1 heaped tsp fresh roasted and ground cumin seeds
4 tbs coconut oil, melted
1 large onion, thinly sliced
3 small peppers, red, green and yellow, sliced
1 cup water

For the Cuban Rice and Beans:

1 medium onion, chopped
1 tbs coconut oil
2 cloves garlic, crushed
2 tsp ground cumin
¾ tsp dried oregano
1 large bay leaf
2 tbs white wine vinegar
1½ tbs tomato purée
1½ tsp salt
350g / 12oz brown Basmati rice
710ml / 1¼ pints chicken stock
1 tin mixed beans, drained
2 tbs freshly chopped parsley

At least 4 hours before you want to cook, slash the skin side of each piece of chicken several times with a sharp knife and put in a bowl. Blend the zests, juices, garlic, salt, and both kinds of cumin until smooth and add one tablespoon of the coconut oil. Blend again to make an emulsion. Pour over the chicken pieces and mix well. Cover and refrigerate. Put 1 tablespoon of coconut oil in a pan and add about ¼ of the mixed pepper slices. Set aside for later. Preheat the oven to 190°C / gas mark 5. In another pan, fry the onion in the rest of the coconut oil for 5 minutes, add the rest of the peppers and fry a little longer. Add the water, bring to the boil and pour into the base of a roasting tin. Place the marinated chicken pieces on top, skin side up, and pour over any remaining marinade. Open roast for about 45 minutes until done. Transfer the chicken, onions, and peppers to a serving dish and keep warm. Pour the remaining juice into a pan and reheat. Briefly stir fry the other peppers. Pour the hot juice over the chicken and top with the mixed peppers. For the rice, fry the onion in the oil until beginning to brown and add the garlic, fry a minute more. Add the cumin, oregano, bay leaf, vinegar, tomato purée, salt and rice and fry another minute. Add the stock and bring to the boil. Simmer for 25 minutes and add the beans. Return to the boil and simmer a further 5 minutes until the rice is soft but al dente. Turn off the heat, cover and leave for 10 minutes, stirring once to distribute the heat. Stir in the parsley and serve.

Dill Chicken

I was inspired to come up with this recipe after a trip to Norway where chicken always seems to be served with a tasty herb coating. The sauce is a herby version of Mary Berry's watercress sauce.

serves 6

6 chicken breast portions
2 tbs olive oil
1 tbs chopped fresh dill
½ tsp chopped fresh thyme
4 cloves garlic, crushed
seasoning

for the sauce:

140ml / ¼ pint milk
140ml / ¼ pint double cream
1 tbs chopped dill
½ tsp chopped fresh thyme
1 tsp plain flour
juice 1 lemon
85g / 3oz butter, melted
1 egg yolk
salt and pepper

Make up a marinade with the olive oil, herbs, garlic and seasoning. Dip the pieces of chicken into the marinade and lay in a baking tin. Cover with foil and leave in the fridge for a few hours. Preheat the oven to 190°C / gas mark 5 and bake the chicken, still covered, for 35 to 45 minutes until done. Put all the sauce ingredients in a tall jug and whizz with a hand blender until frothy. Heat gently in a pan to thicken slightly, stirring all the time. Transfer the chicken pieces to a serving dish and pour the sauce over the top.

Roast Chicken with Honey and Hazelnuts

This is a Yotam Ottolenghi recipe which we have tweaked slightly to suit serving in the Dining Room as a main course. It is quite rich so you can, if you like, serve a smaller portion than usual with plenty of light vegetables and fluffy white rice. The delicious nut, honey and rosewater finish makes it into something really special; it is definitely my favourite chicken recipe.

serves 6

1 large chicken in 12 pieces
2 onions, finely chopped
4 tbs olive oil
1 tsp ground ginger
1 tsp ground cinnamon
2 really good pinches of saffron powder
juice 1 lemon
4 tbs cold water
2 tsp flaked sea salt
½ tsp freshly ground black pepper
110g / 4oz whole hazelnuts
50g / 2oz honey
2 tbs rosewater
1 tsp cornflour
2 spring onions, chopped

In the morning mix the chicken pieces with the onions, olive oil, ginger, cinnamon, saffron, lemon juice, water, salt and pepper. Cover and leave to marinate in the fridge. Make a stock with the carcass and reduce to about 280ml / ½ pint. Preheat the oven to 190°C / gas mark 5.

Transfer the chicken and marinade to a large roasting tray so it fits in on a single layer not too tightly packed. Roast uncovered for 45 minutes until cooked through. Pop the hazels in another tray under the chicken and leave for 10 minutes. Remove, rub off the skins and chop, not too fine, not too rough! You can use a machine if you like but be careful not to over process. When the chicken is ready, melt the honey gently and mix with the rosewater and nuts to make a paste. Place the chicken pieces into your serving dish using a draining spoon and carefully spread a little of the hazelnut mixture on top of each piece. Return to the oven for a few minutes until the nuts are golden. Meanwhile, pour the cooking juice into a pan with the reduced chicken stock. Thicken very slightly with the cornflour and pour this around the chicken. Sprinkle with spring onions.

Coq au Vin

A classic French recipe, ours is adapted from a version by Delia Smith. Traditionally it is cooked on the stove top but we find it easier in the oven. At Doune, it has earned the nickname purple chicken.

serves 8

8 chicken portions, each cut in 2
25g / 1oz butter
1 tbs olive oil
225g / 8oz smoked streaky bacon, chopped
16 button shallots
2 cloves garlic, crushed
2 sprigs fresh thyme
2 bay leaves
1 bottle red wine
freshly ground black pepper
225g / 8oz mushrooms
25g / 1oz butter
25g / 1oz plain flour
seasoning as needed

Fry the chicken pieces in the butter and olive oil, and remove to a roasting tin in a single layer. Preheat the oven to 190°C / gas mark 5. Fry the bacon until crisp and the fat has run out, drain and add to the chicken. Fry the onions in the bacon fat until the outsides are getting golden and add to the chicken with the garlic, thyme and bay. Deglaze with the wine, season with black pepper only and bring to a simmer. Pour this over the chicken and cook in the oven for about 45 minutes until done. Remove the chicken and bits to a serving dish and keep warm. Put the liquid in a pan, add the mushrooms and reduce the liquid to one third. In the meantime, mash the butter and flour together to make a paste. Take the pan off the heat, remove the herbs and sprinkle on the paste. Return to the heat and whisk until thickened. Pour the sauce over the chicken and serve.

Thai Chicken

The paste makes enough for 12 portions but it freezes well for future use. You can use a bought Thai green curry paste if you prefer.

serves 6

1 onion, thinly sliced
1 red pepper, deseeded and thinly sliced
1 tbs coconut oil
6 tbs Thai curry paste
1 tin (385g) coconut milk
3 kaffir lime leaves
seasoning to taste
1 tbs chopped fresh basil
1 tbs chopped fresh coriander
6 portions chicken breast, each cut in 3
1 tsp cornflour

for the Thai paste:

6 green chillies
2 stems lemongrass, rough chopped
2 oz fresh coriander, including stalks
1 inch fresh ginger, peeled and chopped
4 spring onions, rough chopped
3 cloves garlic, peeled and chopped
3 kaffir lime leaves
1 tsp ground cumin
zest and juice 1 lime
¼ pint vegetable stock

Make the Thai paste by blending everything together until smooth. Preheat the oven to 190°C / gas mark 5. Fry the onion and pepper in the coconut oil. Add the 6 tablespoons of paste and cook for one minute.

Add the coconut milk, lime leaves and seasoning and cook for 10 minutes. Place the chicken in a deep roasting tray and pour the mixture over it. Cover with foil and bake for 30 to 40 minutes until done. Remove the chicken pieces to a serving dish and keep warm. Thicken the sauce with the cornflour, stir in the herbs and pour over the chicken.

Toppi's Lemon Chicken

This is a really unusual dish. Try to find leg portions with skin on as the richer meat complements the sweetness and the skin will get caramelised and crisp. The lemon pieces are meant to be eaten, not just a garnish, and they are amazing. It is best served with plenty of plain rice to soak up the sauce.

serves 4

110g / 4oz granulated sugar
1 lemon
4 large chicken leg portions, each cut in 2
salt and pepper
255ml / 9 fl oz water
1 tsp cornflour

Dissolve the sugar in the water and boil for 2 minutes. Pierce the skin of the lemon 3 times with a fork and place in the syrup. Cover and cook for 20 minutes. Remove the lemon and bubble the liquid until it reduces by half and becomes a golden colour. Cut the lemon in 4. Preheat the oven to 190°C / gas mark 5.

Season the chicken really well and place, skin down and in a single layer, in a roasting tin along with the lemon halves. Pour the syrup all over and bake, uncovered, for about 30 minutes. Turn the lemon quarters and chicken pieces over so the skin is now on top, and continue cooking for another 30 minutes. It should be well done and beautifully browned. Place both chicken and lemon in a serving dish and keep warm. Strain the cooking liquid, thicken with the cornflour, check the seasoning, (it can take a lot), and pour it over the chicken.

Cider Baked Chicken

This is very rich but it is super delicious (you can use less cream if you want). It is the strong stock and the cider reduction that gives the intense flavour.

serves 6
1 whole large bulb of garlic
6 chicken portions
25g / 1oz butter
1 tbs garlic infused olive oil
1 can dry cider
150ml / 5 fl oz strong chicken stock
2 bay leaves
175ml / 6 fl oz cream
Seasoning

You can roast the garlic well ahead, any time you have the oven on. Cut the root end off the garlic bulb, wrap loosely in foil, and roast until soft. In a moderate oven, this would take about 20 minutes but slower or faster is fine as long as it is good and soft. Cool, then squeeze the soft garlic out of the skins when required. Preheat the oven to 190°C / gas mark 5. Fry the chicken portions in the butter and garlicky oil to brown the outsides and lay in a deep baking tray in a single layer. Deglaze the pan with a tablespoon of the cider and the stock, pour this over the chicken, season, and bake, uncovered, for about ¾ of an hour. While the chicken is baking, add the rest of the cider, the roasted garlic cloves, and bay leaves to the frying pan. Boil to reduce to about 3 tablespoons. When the chicken is done, remove the pieces to a serving dish, cover and keep warm. Pour the juices into the frying pan and if there is a lot, reduce again. Mash the garlic down with a fork and add the cream, reboil, season to taste, and pour over the chicken pieces.

Fusion Chicken

As soon as Suzanne told me about a roast chicken dish with chorizo under the skin I knew we had to try it. We have made a lot of changes but the original flavours of chorizo and 5 spice are still there. With Italian, French and Asian influences we decided to call it Fusion Chicken. Ready cut portions are easiest, and if you can't find any with the skin on, you can slit the meat and stuff the chorizo inside.

serves 6
6 chicken portions, skin on
110g / 4oz chorizo
25g / 1oz butter
2 tbs strong chicken stock
1 tbs brandy
1 sprig fresh rosemary
1 sprig fresh thyme
seasoning
for the sauce:
140ml / ¼ pint red wine
140ml / ¼ pint strong chicken stock
2 bay leaves
2 sprigs fresh rosemary
2 sprigs fresh thyme
½ level tsp Chinese 5 spice
10g / ½ oz soft butter
10g / ½ oz plain flour
seasoning

Skin and thinly slice the chorizo and place under the skin of the chicken, about 5 or 6 pieces for each portion. Fry the chicken in the butter until golden. Place in a roasting tray big enough to fit all the pieces in one layer with a little gap around each. Deglaze the pan with the stock and brandy and pour this around the chicken. Take the rosemary and thyme leaves from their stalks, roughly chop and sprinkle over the chicken. Season and open roast for about 45 minutes until done. For the sauce, put the wine, bay leaves, rosemary and thyme in the frying pan and bubble to reduce the wine by about half. Add the stock and 5 spice and cook for a few minutes. Remove the bay leaves and herb sprigs. Mash the butter and flour together to make a paste. When ready to serve, put the chicken in your serving dish and keep warm. Pour the cooking juices into the sauce and return to the boil. Take the pan off the heat and sprinkle in the paste, return to the heat and whisk through the boil to thicken. Taste and season if needed. Pour around the chicken and garnish with more sprigs of rosemary and thyme.

Crispy Chicken with Dauphinoise Potatoes

Every so often we come back to this recipe. The aroma as it cooks is wonderful and as guests arrive at the dining room they invariably pop their heads into the kitchen and ask what the incredible smell is. When Ewan was little I needed a recipe for dauphinoise that didn't require too much time in the evenings and came across this one in the Ballymaloe Cookery Course Book. All the preparation is in the morning and all you need to do to serve is put it in the oven for 25 minutes.

serves 6

6 chicken portions, each cut in 2
175g / 6oz fresh white breadcrumbs
1 level tbs dried thyme
1 level tbs dried sage
salt and pepper
2 eggs, well beaten
fat for frying
<u>for the dauphinoise:</u>
floury potatoes
milk
garlic
seasoning
freshly grated nutmeg
double cream

For the dauphinoise, peel and thinly slice enough potatoes to fill a suitable gratin dish for 6 people. Put the potatoes in a pan with enough milk to come halfway up, 1 clove of crushed garlic, plenty of seasoning, and a good grating of nutmeg. Top up with cream to just cover the potatoes. Cook gently, stirring often, until the potato is almost cooked. Spoon into the gratin dish. Bake under the chicken once it has been in for 20 minutes. For the chicken, mix the breadcrumbs with the herbs and a generous amount of salt and pepper. Coat the chicken pieces in egg and then roll in the breadcrumb mix. Preheat the oven to 190°C / gas mark 5. Fry the chicken briefly to set the coating but not brown. Place on a shallow oven tin; a lining of silicon paper helps save on washing up but is not essential. Bake for 45 minutes until the coating is crispy golden and the chicken cooked but still moist.

<u>Variation:</u> **Gratin Potatoes**

2 thinly sliced onions, 25g / 1oz butter, potatoes as above, seasoning, strong home-made beef or chicken stock. Fry the onions in the butter until really well browned. Add the potatoes, seasoning and enough stock to come halfway up the pan. Cook, stirring occasionally until the potatoes are almost cooked. Spoon into the gratin dish and bake as for dauphinoise.

Fragrant Saffron Chicken

This was a Sophie Conran recipe. The colour combination is vibrant and once you add the fresh green parsley at the end it is simply stunning.

serves 6

1 large chicken in 12 pieces
1 tbs olive oil

25g / 1oz butter
2 onions, chopped
2 large cloves garlic, crushed
4cm / 1½ inch ginger, grated
1 tsp ground cumin
1 small butternut squash, peeled, seeded and chopped into 2.5cm / 1 in cubes
3 large tomatoes each cut in 6
large pinch saffron powder
280ml / ½ pint strong chicken stock
2 wide strips lemon zest
2 tbs chopped fresh parsley
¾ tsp salt
freshly ground black pepper

If you can, cut the chicken early and use the carcass to make the stock. Preheat the oven to 190°C / gas mark 5. Heat the oil, fry the chicken pieces quickly and set in a casserole dish. Reduce the heat, add the butter to the frying pan and fry the onions until soft. Stir in the garlic, ginger and cumin, cook for two minutes and add to the casserole with the cut tomatoes. Add the squash to the pan and fry gently for 5 minutes. Stir in the saffron, stock and lemon zest and bring to the boil. Pour this over the chicken, cover, and cook in the oven for 1 hour until done. To serve, spoon the chicken into a serving dish, stir most of the parsley into the juice and pour over the chicken. Sprinkle the rest of the parsley on top.

Sumac Chicken

This is based on a Yotam Ottolenghi recipe and uses the Middle Eastern spice sumac which has a tangy lemony flavour.

serves 6
1 large chicken in 12 pieces
1 large red onion, thinly sliced
2 cloves garlic, crushed
4 tbs olive oil
1 ½ tsp ground allspice
1 tsp ground cinnamon
1 ½ tsp sumac
juice 1 lemon
¼ lemon in very thin half slices
140ml / ¼ pint strong chicken stock
1 flat tsp salt
1 flat tsp cracked black pepper
1 tsp sesame oil
sesame seeds and 2 spring onions to garnish

If you can, cut the chicken early and use the carcass to make a strong stock which you can then use in the marinade. Put all the ingredients, except the garnish, into a large bowl and mix well so that all the chicken pieces are well covered. Cover and leave in the fridge to marinate for at least 4 hours. Preheat the oven to 190°C / gas mark 5. Transfer everything to an oven tray, laying the chicken skin side up, and open roast for about ¾ hour or until the chicken is done. Spoon into a serving dish and sprinkle with the sesame seeds and finely chopped spring onions.

vegetarian

We try to find vegetarian dishes that sit well with the standard main course of the day so the vegetables will likely complement the dish. The Mushroom Bourguignon, for example, is perfect when serving wine based casseroles.

Basil Roulade

This also makes a great starter, use half portions and serve with a mixed salad. The roulade without the filling freezes well, just cut into the sizes required and freeze flat.

serves 4
50g / 2oz butter, melted
50g / 2oz plain flour
250ml / 9 fl oz milk
4 eggs, separated
salt and freshly ground black pepper
20g / ¾oz fresh basil, roughly chopped
vegetarian strong hard cheese, grated
for the filling
175g / 6oz vegetarian cream cheese
85g / 3oz thick natural yoghurt
2 fresh tomatoes, finely diced
20g / ¾ oz fresh basil, roughly chopped
salt and freshly ground black pepper

Preheat the oven to 200°C / gas mark 6. Line a 30x23cm / 12x9in traybake tin with silicon paper, brush with melted butter and sprinkle generously with cheese. Have ready a second piece of paper of the same size, also sprinkled with cheese. Add the flour to the rest of the butter, cook gently for a few minutes and whisk in the milk. Whisking continuously, bring to the boil to thicken and then take off the heat to cool a little. Beat in the egg yolks one at a time and add the basil and seasoning. Whisk the egg whites until really thick and fold into the sauce mixture. Pour into the prepared tin and spread out. Bake for about 15 minutes until the mixture is firm and springs back when touched. Turn out immediately onto the second piece of paper, transfer carefully to a rack, and allow to cool. Beat the filling ingredients together and spread onto the roulade. Roll up and chill well. Using a serrated knife, cut carefully into 8 rings, place onto an ovenproof serving dish and sprinkle with more cheese. Cover with foil and reheat at 200°C / gas mark 6 for 10 minutes only.

Molé

Of all our vegetable stews this rich and flavoursome recipe is my favourite. An aubergine or a small butternut squash can be substituted for the potato.

serves 2

1 onion, chopped
1 clove garlic, crushed
2 tbs olive oil
1 potato, cut into chunks
½ tsp ground cumin
½ tsp ground coriander
½ tsp paprika (or smoked paprika)
¼ tsp chilli powder
salt and pepper
1 tin tomatoes
½ the tomato tin of water
1 tsp tomato purée
1 tin red kidney beans, drained and washed
110g / 4oz button mushrooms, sliced
12g / ½ oz dark chocolate
1 tbs lime juice
1 tbs fresh coriander leaves, roughly chopped

Fry the onion and garlic in the oil until softened. Add the potato (or vegetable) and spices, and cook gently for a few minutes. Add the seasoning, tomatoes, pureé and water and cook until the potato is just soft. Add the beans and cook a few more minutes. Add the mushrooms, chocolate and lime, and heat through. Take off the heat, mix in the coriander and serve with rice or mashed potatoes.

Lemony Chickpea Broth

This was served to me by my niece a few years ago and I loved it. It is very unusual and is always a huge success. If you want to make your own harissa paste, our recipe is on page 25.

serves 2

1 tbs olive oil
1 medium onion, diced
4 cloves garlic, crushed
1 can chickpeas, drained
1 level tsp ground cumin
1 tsp harissa paste
430ml / ¾ pint vegetable stock
juice of one lemon
2 thick slices of bread, torn into pieces
2 eggs
6 capers, drained and chopped fine
4 olives, drained and chopped fine
2 teaspoons harissa paste
strips of roast red peppers (optional)
2 tablespoons of coarsely chopped fresh flat parsley or coriander

Fry the onion in the oil until soft. Add the garlic and cook gently for a minute or so more. Add the chickpeas, cumin, harissa, stock and lemon juice, and simmer for 5 minutes. Start poaching the eggs. Put the bread in large soup bowls, ladle over the broth and place a poached egg on top of each. Top each with the chopped capers and olives and a teaspoon of harissa paste. Add the pepper strips if using and sprinkle generously with parsley or coriander.

Sweet and Sour Sauce

This is a wonderful, zingy sauce invented by Mary a long time ago. It is the perfect foil for mixed roast vegetables, egg and breadcrumbed sliced aubergines or battered onion rings.

serves 6

coarse grated zest 1 orange
coarse grated zest 1 lemon
1 red pepper, sliced
1 tbs olive oil
1 tin (240g) apricots in light syrup
juice 1 orange
140ml / ¼ pint white wine vinegar
1 tbs chopped stem ginger in syrup
175g / 6oz sugar
1 tsp cornflour
1 dsp English mustard powder

Fry the grated citrus and sliced pepper in the oil until soft. Quarter the apricots and add these and the juice from the tin with everything else except the cornflour and mustard to the pan. Simmer for 5 minutes. Mix the cornflour and mustard powder with a little water and use to thicken the sauce. Serve with your chosen vegetable and rice.

Mushroom Bourguignon

serves 2

2 tbs olive oil
2 medium onions, roughly chopped
1 large carrot, roughly chopped
1 clove garlic, crushed
1 tsp tomato purée
2 tsp plain flour
140ml / ¼ pint red wine
1 sprig fresh rosemary
2 sprigs fresh thyme
140ml / ¼ pint vegetable stock
450g / 1lb button mushrooms
20g / ¾ oz butter

Fry the onions and carrot in the oil, add the garlic, purée, and flour and cook for 1 minute. Add the red wine, stock and herbs, and simmer for about 15 minutes. Fry the mushrooms in the butter, add to the pan and simmer for 5 minutes.

Croustade

This is based on a Rose Elliot recipe. It makes a great alternative to a roast as it goes really well with roast potatoes and the sauce means you don't need a separate gravy.

serves 4

110g / 4oz soft white breadcrumbs
110g / 4oz ground almonds
50g / 2oz softened butter
50g / 2oz flaked almonds
50g / 2oz roast hazels, skinned and chopped
1 clove garlic, crushed
3 tbs mixed fresh herbs
sauce for topping.

Preheat the oven to 180°C / gas mark 4. Mix the crumbs and ground almonds and rub in the butter. Add the nuts, garlic and herbs. Spread to just under half fill an ovenproof serving dish. Bake for about 15 minutes until slightly browned and crispy. Make a bechamel sauce of whatever flavour you like and pour it on top when ready to serve.

curries

When we first started, we used to do lots of curry nights and, in the typical Doune style, they were big buffet events with lots of different dishes. These days we don't get the opportunity very often. Most people have access to fantastic Indian restaurants and there are masses of wonderful books and recipes online making every home cook a curry expert, so there has to be a very good reason for us to join the fray. When we do, it just doesn't seem right not to include these four favourites. All the recipes yield 12 small portions as part of a large mixed buffet.

Punjabi Bean and Lentil Stew

A lovely mild and creamy curry to contrast the heat in other dishes.

1 can red kidney beans
2 tbs puy lentils, cooked al dente
25g / 1oz fresh ginger, peeled and finely chopped
½ tsp salt
juice 1 lemon
½ tsp garam masala
1 tsp tomato purée
1 clove garlic, crushed
1 pinch cayenne pepper
25g / 1oz butter
½ tsp sugar
4 tbs double cream

Drain and rinse the beans. In water to cover, simmer the beans and lentils with the ginger for 5 minutes and then drain. Mash them up slightly but leave some whole beans and lentils for texture. Add the rest of the ingredients and simmer gently for a few minutes then turn off the heat and leave to infuse until ready to reheat and serve.

Mary's Fruit Curry

We have often been asked for this fruit curry recipe. Invented by Mary, it is an unusual, mildly spiced dish. It does make a lot but, since it freezes very well, it doesn't seem worth making less.

coarse grated zest 1 orange
coarse grated zest 2 lemons
4 carrots, grated
25g / 1oz fresh ginger, peeled and grated
1 tbs oil or ghee
2 apples, peeled and chopped
½ small melon, peeled and chopped
10 dates, chopped
8 dried apricots, chopped
flesh 1 orange, chopped
2 tbs sultanas
2 tbs tandoori spice mix
560ml / 1 pint yoghurt
juice 1 lemon
2 bananas

Fry the zests, carrots and ginger in the fat. Add the apples and fry until softening. Add the melon, dates, apricots, sultanas, orange, and tandoori mix and fry for a further 5 minutes. Add the yoghurt and lemon juice and simmer for 5 minutes. Add the bananas, cook one minute more. Leave to mature for a few hours. Re-heat gently, stirring often

Aubergine in Pickling Style

Based on a Madhur Jaffrey recipe we often use this as a vegetarian main course as well as part of a curry night. It is rich but fresh tasting and looks stunning with a bright glossy sauce studded with shiny black aubergine.

2 large aubergines in thick slices
salt
oil or ghee
5cm / 2 in cube fresh ginger, peeled and chopped fine
12 large cloves garlic, peeled
112ml / 4 fl oz water
2 tsp whole fennel seeds
1 tsp whole cumin seeds
2 tins tomatoes
2 dsp ground coriander
1 tsp paprika
2 tbs fresh coriander leaves

Sprinkle the aubergine slices with salt and leave to weep. Wash, dry and fry until soft. Blend the ginger, garlic and water to make a paste. Fry the fennel and cumin seeds in 6 tablespoons of oil or ghee until turning brown and add the tomato, ginger and garlic mixture and the rest of the spices. Stir and cook gently for 5 minutes. Add the aubergine, cover, and cook for 5 to 10 minutes. Top with the coriander.

Hot Cabbage and Carrot Curry

With us right from the start, this comes from An Indian Housewife's Recipe Book by Laxmi Khurana which is full of lovely family recipes that you won't find in restaurants. The key ingredient is asafoetida and there is something magical about it. Once it hits the hot fat the smell is just amazing, filling the kitchen with rich, authentic aromas. Extra cayenne makes it really hot without overpowering the other flavours. This dish freezes well.

2 tbs oil or ghee
¼ tsp whole cumin seeds
¼ tsp whole black mustard seeds
¼ tsp asafoetida
4 green chillies, chopped
¼ medium white cabbage, thinly shredded
4 small carrots, grated
1 tsp sugar
½ tsp salt
½ tsp ground turmeric
cayenne to taste, optional
2 tsp tomato purée
3 tbs water
1 tbs lemon juice

Heat the fat and add the cumin, mustard and asafoetida. Cook for a few seconds but do not burn. Add the rest except the purée, water and lemon juice and stir-fry for 2 minutes. Add the rest, cover and simmer for about 10 minutes.

Puddings

Pudding choices through the week will invariably include a tart, a Pavlova, ice cream or sorbet, some Doune fruit and, of course, chocolate. I have often been told that I have too many chocolate recipes, but I'm sure that can't be possible!

Blackcurrant and Red Wine Jelly with Elderflower Cream

It is always great to find a good recipe that uses our beautiful homegrown fruit and this one is very good indeed. The rich, intensely flavoured jelly is incredible and set off perfectly by the light elderflower cream. It is fun to set the jellies in individual glasses at an angle. We grow stunning little viola flowers which are edible and make a wonderful decoration. Thanks are due to one of our guests who gave us this idea in a recipe swap.

serves 6 to 8
350g / 12oz blackcurrants
125g / 4½ oz caster sugar
225ml / 8 fl oz light and fruity red wine
85ml / 3 fl oz water
4 sheets leaf gelatin
for the elderflower cream:
45ml / 1½ fl oz whole milk
200ml / 7 fl oz double cream
20g / ¾ oz caster sugar
3½ tbs elderflower cordial
115ml / 4 fl oz natural yoghurt

Put the blackcurrants, sugar, wine and water in a pan and simmer gently for 15 minutes. Put through a sieve and leave to drain for at least an hour, do not squeeze. Soak the gelatin leaves in a bowl of cold water for 5 minutes. Warm the blackcurrant juice slightly, lift the gelatin out of the water, squeeze gently and add to the juice. Stir until dissolved and pour into your serving dish or glasses. Cool and chill to set.

When ready to serve, whisk the milk, cream and sugar together until lightly whipped. Stir in the elderflower and yoghurt. Spoon onto the set jelly and decorate.

Gooseberry Meringue Cake

You can use any cooked fruit for this as long as it is quite tart.

serves 8
for the sponge:
150g / 5oz caster sugar
150g / 5oz soft butter
2 eggs
3 egg yolks
85g / 3oz ground almonds
50g / 2oz self-raising flour
1 tsp baking powder
for the filling:
350g / 12oz tart gooseberries
140ml / ¼ pint water
sugar to taste
1 dsp cornflour
for the meringue:
3 egg whites
175g / 6oz granulated sugar

Line a 23cm / 9in cake tin with silicon paper. Find an oven proof dish that this size cake will fit in snugly, a fluted flan dish is ideal. Preheat the oven to 180°C / gas mark 4. To make the sponge, beat the sugar and butter together until light and fluffy. Beat in the eggs, yolks and ground almonds. Sift the flour and baking powder into the bowl and fold in gently. Pour into the cake tin and bake for 20 to 30 minutes until just done. Turn out and cool on a wire rack. Cook the gooseberries gently in the water until just beginning to break down but some are still whole. Sweeten with sugar but leave it quite sharp. Thicken with cornflour and leave to cool. Preheat the oven to 170°C / gas mark 3. Put the sponge into the serving dish and spread the gooseberries on top. To make the meringue, whisk the egg whites until stiff and gradually whisk in all the sugar. Spread this on top, making sure the meringue touches the edge of the dish to seal in the cake and fruit. Bake for 15-20 mins until just browning. Turn off the oven but leave the cake in until completely cold allowing the meringue to crisp up.

Sherry Trifle

On roast night we almost always serve a trifle. This was my dad's favourite pudding and I insist on making it just as mum used to. You can, if you like, use sponge fingers instead of making the sponge but this is a classic and sophisticated dessert so absolutely and categorically no tinned fruit or jelly!

serves 4 to 6

2 eggs
50g / 2oz caster sugar
50g / 2oz plain flour, sifted
good quality raspberry jam
up to 6 tbs sweet sherry
2 egg yolks
1 dsp caster sugar
¼ tsp vanilla extract
1 tsp cornflour
280ml / ½ pint milk
175ml / 6 fl oz double cream
1 tbs toasted flaked almonds

Preheat the oven to 220°C / gas mark 7. Line a 30x23cm / 12x9in traybake tin with silicon paper. Whisk the eggs and sugar until thick. Gently fold in the flour and spread into the tin. Bake for about 8 minutes until it springs back when touched. Turn on to a rack straight away, remove the paper and leave to cool. Cut the sponge in half. Spread one half with the jam and put the other half on top to make a sandwich. Cut into squares and place these in a serving bowl. Soak with plenty of sherry so that it is moist to the touch. Whisk the egg yolks, sugar and vanilla in a bowl until the eggs have turned paler. Blend the cornflour in the milk and bring to the boil, stirring all the time. Pour this onto the yolk mixture, whisking constantly. Return to the pan and heat carefully again, stirring all the time, until the custard coats the back of a spoon. Pour over the sponge and leave to cool. Lightly whip the cream, spread over the custard and sprinkle with the toasted almonds.

Variation: Limoncello Trifle

Use lemon curd instead of jam and limoncello instead of sherry. Substitute the zest of 1 lemon for vanilla in the custard.

Chocolate Brownie Pudding

No excuses, this is rich and chocolatey. It does make a lot but I don't think a lot is really a problem! You can substitute toasted hazelnuts for the walnuts if you like. If you prefer to serve a separate, runny chocolate sauce instead of the thick topping, use the same ingredients but boil the syrup for one minute only.

serves 10

125g / 4½ oz walnuts
350g / 12oz dark (70%) chocolate
250g / 9oz unsalted butter
50g / 2oz plain flour
1 tsp baking powder
3 eggs
125g / 4½ oz soft brown sugar
icing sugar to dredge
Glossy Chocolate Topping:
50g / 2oz sugar
1 tbs water
95g / 3½ oz dark (70%) chocolate
10g / ½ oz unsalted butter
1 tbs brandy

Preheat the oven to 190°C / gas mark 5. Line a 25cm / 10in clip or loose based tin with silicon paper. In a heavy-based pan, toast the walnuts lightly and chop very roughly. Melt the chocolate and butter in a bowl over a pan of hot water and cool slightly. Sift the flour and baking powder together. Preheat the oven to 180°C / gas mark 4. Whisk the eggs and sugar until thick and mousse-like. Gently fold the chocolate into the egg mixture. Fold in the flour and nuts and turn into the tin. Bake for 35 minutes. It should be barely firm. Cool in the tin, it may sink a little but this is good. To make the topping, boil the sugar and water for 3 minutes. Cool a little and add the chocolate and butter. Beat well and add the brandy. It should be thick and glossy. Remove the brownie from the tin and place on a serving plate. Dredge very heavily with icing sugar. Top with the thick chocolate mixture in lines to give a stripy effect. Serve with a fifty/fifty mix of whipped cream and natural yoghurt, for 10 we would use 280ml / ½ pint of each.

Kristy's Rhubarb Flan

Airor resident Kristy cooked with us for the 2008 season and gave us this 'never fails' rhubarb recipe. It should be made well ahead for maximum chilling time.

serves 10

900g / 2lb fresh rhubarb
sugar to taste
110g / 4oz plain flour
110g / 4oz butter, melted
1 egg
85g / 3oz sugar
1½ tsp baking powder
1 tsp vanilla extract
for the topping:
450g / 1lb sour cream
85g / 3oz sugar
1½ tbs cornflour, sieved
2 egg yolks
1 tsp vanilla extract
for the cream:
110ml / 4 fl oz double cream

110ml / 4 fl oz natural yoghurt
grated nutmeg

Cook the rhubarb so it is soft, and sweeten to taste. Line a 25cm / 10in clip tin with silicon paper. Preheat the oven to 175°C / gas mark 3 to 4. Mix together the next six ingredients and press into the tin. Spread the rhubarb on top. Beat the topping ingredients together and pour over the fruit. Bake for 1 hour. Cool in the tin and chill well. Turn out onto a plate and then invert onto your serving plate. Whip the cream and stir in the yoghurt. Spread over the flan and generously grate nutmeg over the top.

Variation:

Apple and Raspberry Flan

Use apple purée and fresh or frozen raspberries. Omit the nutmeg and decorate with apple slices and fresh raspberries, or sprinkle with freeze dried raspberry powder.

Sticky Toffee Pudding

I often think we shouldn't serve this as it really is ubiquitous. However, it is massively popular and we are frequently asked for the recipe, so we keep coming back to our version of this modern classic. It is a good idea to let the pudding cool for a few minutes before pouring on the sauce, as the extra heat from the dish can cause it to bubble over, making a very sticky mess!

serves 8
175g / 6oz stoned dates, chopped
1 tsp bicarbonate of soda
1 tsp vanilla extract
280ml / ½ pint boiling water
50g / 2oz soft butter
175g / 6oz granulated sugar
1 egg
225g / 8oz plain flour
1 tsp baking powder
for the sauce:
150g / 5oz soft brown sugar
85g / 3oz butter
4 tbs double cream

Put the dates, bicarbonate of soda and vanilla in a bowl, add the boiling water and leave to steep for 2 hours. Preheat the oven to 190°C / gas mark 5. Beat the butter and sugar together until light and fluffy and beat in the egg. Sieve the flour with the baking powder. Gently mix everything together, pour the batter into a 1.85 litre / 3¼ pint shallow ovenproof dish and bake for 40 minutes until springy to the touch. Remove from the oven. Heat the sauce ingredients gently in a pan and simmer for 3 minutes. Pour this over the pudding and serve with plenty of pouring cream or custard.

Variation:

Sticky Ginger Pudding

Halve the amount of vanilla extract. Add 2 teaspoons of ground ginger and 1 tablespoon of chopped stem ginger to the sponge. Stir a tablespoon of the stem ginger syrup into the topping sauce once it has simmered.

Eccles Cakes

These can be served as a simple finger pudding with coffee or with the orange sauce that goes with our clootie dumpling on page 87. The mint and currant version, which came from my mother in law, is lovely with cream whipped with a dash of elderflower cordial. Eccles Cakes can be frozen uncooked; best to defrost before baking. Our puff pastry recipe is on page 160.

serves 8

puff pastry using 175g / 6oz flour
40g / 1½ oz butter
40g / 1½ oz demerara sugar
6 tbs currants
2 tbs mixed peel
a good grating of nutmeg
milk to brush
sugar to sprinkle

Melt the butter and sugar and stir in the fruit and nutmeg. Cool. Preheat the oven to 220°C / gas mark 7. Roll the pastry and cut into eight squares each 6cm / 3.5in and brush all the edges with milk. Make piles of the filling in the centre of each square. Pull the edges together to form a bag, seal well and turn over. Roll lightly to make circles. Slash each one 3 times, brush with milk and sprinkle with sugar. Bake for 20 minutes until puffy and golden. Cool briefly before lifting onto a rack. Serve warm.

Variation: Fresh Mint Eccles

Omit the peel and nutmeg. Use 8 tablespoons of currants and 1 of freshly chopped sweet mint.

Chocolate Orange Pudding

The centre of the pudding will be sunken but don't be tempted to cook it longer to make it rise as this will overcook the eggs and give a grainy texture. The pudding should be moist and silky smooth.

serves 8 to 10

225g / 8oz dark chocolate (70%)
zest and juice 1 large orange
175g / 6oz unsalted butter, cut into chunks
150g / 5oz sugar
4 eggs
2 large oranges in segments
2 tbs Grand Marnier
225ml / 8 fl oz double cream
grated chocolate to decorate

Line a 900g / 2lb loaf tin with silicon paper. Melt a little of the butter and brush the paper well. Preheat the oven to 180°C / gas mark 4. In a heavy-based pan, melt the chocolate gently with the grated rind and juice. Add the butter and sugar and continue to heat gently until melted. Remove from the heat and whisk in the eggs one at a time. Pour into the prepared tin and bake for 45 minutes. Cool in the tin and chill well. Pour the Grand Marnier over the orange segments and chill for at least 30 minutes. To assemble: Pull the paper off the pudding and place on a serving plate. Strain the juice from the orange slices and pile them on top of the pudding. Mix the strained juice with the cream and whip lightly. Use this to cover the pudding and sprinkle with chocolate.

Variation: **Mocha Pudding**

Substitute 175ml / 6 fl oz strong black coffee for the orange zest and juice. Don't use the orange segments. Add 2 tbs milk, 1½ tbs caster sugar and ½ tsp vanilla extract to the cream.

Ginger and Orange Torte

Using the whole orange gives a really intense flavour. It doesn't seem worth making the orange pulp in small amounts so the quantity given here should make enough for two cakes; the excess can be frozen for future use. The cake keeps well but both the syrups lose flavour very quickly so should be made fresh.

serves 6

for the orange pulp:

3 medium oranges

for the Torte:

225g / 8oz orange pulp
150g / 5oz ground almonds
150g / 5oz caster sugar
1 tsp baking powder
3 eggs
1 egg yolk

for the ginger and orange syrup:

5cm / 2in fresh ginger, peeled and grated
zest 1 orange
110g / 4oz sugar
280ml / ½ pint water
1½ tbs chopped stem ginger

Prepare the pulp by pricking the oranges 3 times with a fork and pressure cooking with 560ml / 1 pint of water at high pressure for 8 minutes. (Or cover with water and simmer for 1 ½ to 2 hours until soft.) Drain, remove any pips, and process, skin and all, in a food processor until smooth. Preheat the oven to 170°C / gas mark 3. Line a 20cm / 8in cake tin with silicon paper. Place the ground almonds, sugar and baking powder in a large bowl and rub between the fingers to remove any lumps. Whisk the eggs thoroughly. Mix all together to make a thick batter and pour into the tin. Bake for 40 to 50 minutes until just firm. Cool in the tin. To make the syrup, heat the ginger, zest, sugar and water in a pan and boil for 15 minutes or until syrupy. Strain into another pan and add the chopped stem ginger. When ready to serve, warm the torte gently in a low oven and turn out onto a serving plate with a lip. Warm the syrup and drizzle it on top. Serve with cream.

Variations:

Orange and Rosemary Torte

For the syrup, instead of the ginger, orange and stem ginger, use 1 tablespoon of well-crushed fresh rosemary spikes. You may not need the full quantity of syrup. Spikes of rosemary and borage flowers make a stunning decoration.

Chocolate Orange Torte

Instead of a syrup, top the cold torte with a ganache. Bring 110g / 4oz double cream to simmer and pour on 110g / 4oz dark chocolate and the zest of an orange. Stir until smooth, cool slightly and spread over the torte.

Black Beer, Beetroot and Chocolate Pudding

We use our local beer Skye Black for this, but any dark beer or stout will give the sweetness and depth of flavour that is needed. The beetroot makes the pudding moist and rich. You can leave it out for a lighter result.

serves 8
150g / 5oz beetroot
50g / 2oz cocoa, sifted
110g / 4oz dark muscovado sugar
250ml / ½ pint Skye Black beer
2 tsp vanilla
225g / 8oz plain flour
½ tsp baking powder
½ tsp bicarb
125g / 4½ oz soft unsalted butter
150g / 5oz caster sugar
2 eggs, beaten
for the topping:
85ml / 3 fl oz water
25g / 1oz dark Muscovado sugar
85g / 3oz unsalted butter
150g / 5oz dark (70%) chocolate

Peel and finely grate the beetroot. Preheat the oven to 180°C / gas mark 4. Mix the cocoa with the muscovado sugar. Bring the beer to the boil, pour onto the cocoa mixture and add the vanilla. Stir well to dissolve. Sift the flour with the raising agents. Beat the butter with the sugar until light and fluffy then stir in the prepared flour and eggs until well mixed. Stir in the cocoa mix and beetroot. Pour into a shallow 1.85 litre / 3¼ pint ovenproof dish and bake for about 45 minutes until springy to the touch. Gently heat the topping ingredients until melted, pour over the pudding and serve with pouring cream.

Mocha Pots

One of Martin's recipes. They are rich so a small ramekin is a good portion. The orange version is like molten Terry's Chocolate Orange!

serves 6
85ml / 3 fl oz milk
1 dsp fresh ground coffee beans
200ml / 7 fl oz double cream
200g / 7oz dark chocolate
1 egg, beaten
85ml / 3 fl oz double cream
1 tbs brandy or Drambuie
chocolate for grating

Heat the milk close to the boil and pour on to the coffee grounds. Leave to infuse for 30 minutes. Melt the chocolate over hot water. Strain the coffee into a bowl and add the cream. Whisk to blend well but not to thicken. Add the egg and whisk again. Add one-third of the chocolate and whisk until smooth then add the rest. Whisk again and divide between 6 ramekins. Cool and refrigerate. Whisk the cream and brandy divide between the pots and decorate with grated chocolate.

Variation:

Chocolate Orange Pots

Replace the milk with orange juice and the coffee with the zest of 1 large orange. No need to heat or infuse. Use Grand Marnier in the cream.

Clootie Dumpling

This traditional gem of a recipe was given to me by a friend when I moved to the Highlands 38 years ago and first discovered Dumplings. I added the orange sauce for serving in the dining room. The cloot is a cloth and needs to be at least 60cm / 2 ft square. Old sheeting or double thickness muslin is fine, but have it and some string to tie ready before you start. This is a standard size dumpling which feeds up to 20. Just warm up the number of slices you require on a baking try covered with foil. The rest can either be used as cake, crumbled into ice cream, or fried for breakfast. Slices also freeze very successfully. This is Andy's favourite pudding.

Makes 18 to 20 slices
flour to sprinkle
450g / 1lb self-raising flour
450g / 1lb raisins
225g / 8oz beef suet
225g / 8oz sugar
3 tsp mixed spice
1 tsp bicarbonate of soda
½ tsp salt
3 dsp black treacle
milk to mix

Orange Sauce (for 6)
zest and juice 1 orange
25g / 1oz butter
25g / 1oz plain flour
sugar to taste
more orange juice as required
glug of Grand Marnier (optional)

Set a very large pan of water to boil. Scald the cloot in boiling water and lay it in a medium-size bowl. Sprinkle lightly with flour. In another bowl, mix all the other ingredients together to make a stiff, smooth mixture and spoon into the cloth. Sprinkle the top with more flour. Gather the cloot around the mixture and tie with string leaving a little room for expansion. Lower carefully into boiling water. Bring back to the boil and simmer very gently for 3 hours. Prepare a large bowl with cold water. Lift out the dumpling and dip it into the water for 30 seconds. Place on a plate and undo the cloot, pulling down the sides of the cloth. Invert another plate on top and turn the whole thing over. Carefully remove the rest of the cloot. Heat the oven to 140°C / gas mark 1 and turn off. Put the dumpling into the oven and leave to dry out. Traditionally this would have been done on the hearth.

For the sauce: Make a roux with the butter and flour, add the zest and cook gently. Stir in the juice and, stirring, bring to the boil to make a thin, smooth sauce. Add the Grand Marnier and sweeten to taste.

To reheat the pudding: Preheat the oven to 170°C / gas mark 3. Cut slices and place on a baking tray. Cover with foil and place in the oven for about 15 minutes. Serve with the sauce and pouring cream.

Cinnamon Apple Crunch

This is a traditional Norwegian pudding, the translation of which is Lady with a Veil. It is light and delicate after a big main course. This was the first time we used the cream and yoghurt mix which makes an altogether lighter and fresher topping than just cream and we have used it a lot since. Layering it up at the last minute means the crumbs stay crunchy but I believe the traditional way is to make it in advance and have everything soft. We try to make as many thin layers as possible, which look stunning in a glass dish.

serves 8

60g / 2½ oz butter
150g / 5 oz fresh white breadcrumbs
2 level tsp cinnamon
95g / 3½ oz soft brown sugar (half dark, half light)
4 large cooking apples
4 tbs water
1 tbs sugar
200ml / 7 fl oz double cream
2 tbs caster sugar
200ml / 7 fl oz natural yoghurt

Melt the butter in a heavy-based pan and stir in the breadcrumbs, cinnamon and brown sugar. Cook gently, stirring often, until crisp and toffee like. Cool. Peel, core and slice the apples and poach with the water until soft. Add the one tablespoon of sugar and purée. Cool and chill. Whip the cream with the caster sugar and stir in the yoghurt. Layer in a serving dish finishing with cream and decorate with a tiny sprinkling of cinnamon. Serve straight away.

Variations:

Ginger Gooseberry Crunch

Use 450g / 1lb gooseberries instead of apple, it may need a little more sugar but be careful not to over sweeten. Use ginger instead of cinnamon

Nutmeg Rhubarb Crunch

Use 450g / 1lb rhubarb, cooked, and 225g / 8oz fresh strawberries instead of apple and substitute nutmeg for the cinnamon.

Fruit Pie

The fruit mixture was inspired by a Delia Smith compote recipe. It is wickedly good as a pie. Our puff pastry recipe is on page 160 or if you prefer flaky pastry this is on page 161.

serves 6

175g / 6oz mixed dried fruit salad
110g / 4oz large juicy raisins
1 orange
140ml / ¼ pint port
puff pastry using 175g / 6oz flour

Roughly chop the larger pieces of dried fruit. Add water to just cover, bring gently to the boil and simmer for 10 minutes. Remove the zest from half the orange and cut into thin strips. Now remove all the pith, slice the flesh into rounds and cut each round into 4. Add the orange slices, zest and raisins to the pan and continue to simmer for 15 minutes. Remove from the heat and add the port and juice from the other half of the orange. Transfer to a pie dish, cover and leave to cool and steep for at least 5 hours. Preheat the oven to 220°C / gas mark 7. Roll the pastry to fit the pie dish and place on a lined baking tray. When you put the pastry in the oven, put the pie dish in on the bottom shelf. Bake for 20 to 25 minutes. When the pastry is risen and brown, lift it onto the fruit.

Profiteroles

Light and delicate, profiteroles fit with all sorts of fillings and sauces. The possibilities are near infinite but these are our favourites.

serves 6 (3 small buns per person)

Our method for the profiteroles:

Make up the choux pastry as on page 166. Preheat the oven to 200°C / gas mark 6. Place teaspoonfulls on a lined baking tray. Bake for 20 to 25 minutes. Reduce the heat to 180°C / gas mark 4, move any darker buns to the middle and cook for a further 5 minutes. Prick each bun with a sharp knife to let out the steam and return to the oven for a few more minutes. They should be quite crisp, but on the other hand, you don't want them too hard. Cool on a rack and cover with a clean tea towel until required. Make your filling and sauce. Cut each bun open and spoon in some filling. Once they are all filled, layer up in a serving bowl, alternating buns and sauce.

<u>for Rich Chocolate:</u>

175g / 6oz dark (70%) chocolate
14g / ½ oz butter
1 tbs double cream
1 tbs Drambuie
4 tbs water
250ml / 9 fl oz double cream, whipped

Put the chocolate, butter, first lot of cream, Drambuie and water in a heatproof bowl. Place over boiling water and turn off the heat. Leave until melted and stir to combine. Fill the buns with the cream and layer with the warm sauce.

<u>for Lemon Toffee:</u>

250ml / 9 fl oz double cream, whipped
6 dsp lemon curd (page 128)
½ the sticky toffee sauce recipe (page 83)

Fill each bun with cream and a small amount of lemon curd. Layer with hot toffee sauce.

<u>for Apple Pie:</u>

Apple purée, cream and Calvados filling. Sticky toffee sauce (page 83) with cinnamon and walnuts.

Syllabub and Brandy Snaps

The syllabub is an Elizabeth David recipe that I have been using since I was first married. Unlike many, it doesn't separate so can be made well in advance. It can be a bit splashy so choose a big bowl!

serves 6 to 8
for the syllabub:
110ml / 4 fl oz sweet white wine or sherry
2 tbs brandy
rind and juice 1 lemon
50g / 2oz caster sugar
280ml / ½ pint double cream
for the brandy snaps:
25g / 1oz butter
25g / 1oz sugar
25g / 1oz golden syrup
25g / 1oz plain flour
1 tsp brandy

For the syllabub, mix the first four ingredients in a large bowl and leave to meld for an hour. Slowly pour in the cream, stirring all the time. Whisk until it holds shape, (it can take a while), transfer to individual dishes or glasses and chill. To make the brandy snaps preheat the oven to 200°C / gas mark 6 and line two baking trays with silicon paper. Have ready two wooden spoons. Gently melt the butter, sugar and syrup and add the flour and brandy. It will be quite runny but don't be tempted to add more flour! Drop well-spaced teaspoonfuls of mixture onto the trays and bake one tray at a time for about 5 minutes. The snaps should be brown and bubbling. Take out and leave to cool for a minute. Working quickly, peel off a snap and shape it around a wooden spoon. Leave it on and shape the next around the second spoon. The first snap should now be set. Pull it off and repeat. If biscuits get too crisp to roll put the tray back in the oven for a few seconds and they will soften (not too long or they will burn). Once cooled, keep in an airtight container until ready to serve.

Fruit Financiers

When diners ask us why these are called financiers the answer is 'because they are very rich!'. It makes for a bit of fun but I think the name really comes from the original cakes being baked in rectangular moulds that looked like gold bars. We find individual ones work well, but it is a bit fiddly and for speed you could cook the mixture in a large dish. (Cooking time may be longer.) They can be prepared in the morning and cooked when needed.

serves 6 to 8
125g / 4½ oz slightly salted butter
25g / 1oz caster sugar
50g / 2oz soft brown sugar
125g / 4½ oz ground almonds
25g / 1oz plain flour
25g / 1oz runny honey
3 egg whites
25g / 1oz caster sugar
150g / 5oz fresh berries

Melt the butter and use some to brush the insides of the ramekins. Add the honey to the pan and leave to cool slightly. Preheat the oven to 200°C / gas mark 6. Mix the sugars, almonds and flour together. Whip the egg whites to stiff peaks and whisk in the second lot of caster sugar. Mix the butter and honey into the dry ingredients and fold in the egg whites carefully. Fold in the fruit and fill the ramekins almost to the top. Cook for about 25 minutes until risen and golden. Allow a few minutes to cool down before serving as they are very hot. Serve with cream whipped with a dash of Drambuie.

Variations: **Apple Financiers**

Peel, core and chop 2 eating apples and open roast with a little sugar and apple juice at 200°C / gas mark 6 for about 20 minutes. Cool and use instead of the berries. Calvados is lovely in the cream.

Chocolate Financiers

Use dark chocolate chips instead of the berries.

Cappuccino Crème Brûlée

After various attempts at finding a good crème brûlée recipe I saw this idea for the caramel by Mary Berry a few years ago and we haven't looked back. You can leave out the coffee if you want.

serves 8

5 large egg yolks
40g / 1½ oz caster sugar
½ tsp vanilla extract
560ml / 1 pint double cream
2½ tsp coffee granules
85g / 3oz caster sugar for the caramel

Preheat the oven to 170°C / gas mark 3. Whisk the yolks, sugar and vanilla until smooth. Heat the cream until it is just starting to bubble around the edges of the pan, take off the heat and sprinkle in the coffee. Stir until dissolved. Pour on to the yolk mixture whisking well. Sieve into a jug and pour into 8 ramekins. Place in a bain-marie using boiling water to halfway up the dishes. Bake for 30 minutes until softly set, they should still be wobbling. Remove from the water, cool and chill. For the caramel: Have ready a tin lined with silicon paper. Put the sugar in a heavy-based pan and dampen with a couple of tablespoons of water. Dissolve over a low heat. Turn the heat up to moderate and cook until straw colour. Pour immediately onto the tin and cool. Crack up and blitz in a food processor until fine. Keep in an airtight container. An hour before serving, preheat the grill until really hot. Spread a teaspoon of the caramel on each brûlée and cook as near to the element/flame as possible for 2 to 3 minutes until the sugar has melted again. Chill, but bring to room temperature to serve.

Variation: **Crema Catalana**

Not the traditional method for this classic Spanish pudding but it works really well. Omit the coffee. Add a ¼ tsp cinnamon and the grated zest of an orange to the cream before you scald it.

Fruit Compote and Coconut Cream

You can use any combination of fruit you like for this, apples, pears, plums, peaches, nectarines and rhubarb are all good. The softer and riper the fruit the faster it will cook. Dark plums add a particularly good colour to the juice. You can substitute fresh lemon and lime zest for the lemongrass and lime leaves if you want.

Serves 6 to 8
3tbs sweet dessert wine and 3tbs white wine
125g / 4½ oz demerara sugar
1 stalk lemongrass, split down the middle and bruised
2 crushed kaffir lime leaves
2cm / ¾ in fresh ginger, peeled and finely sliced
3 dessert apples, peeled, cored and quartered
3 pears, peeled, cored and quartered
6 dark plums, halved and stoned
<u>for the Coconut Cream</u>
½ standard 385g tin coconut milk
1½ tbs sugar
½ tsp cornflour
140ml / ¼ pint double cream

Preheat the oven to 190°C / gas mark 5. Put the first 5 ingredients in a pan and warm to melt the sugar. Lay the prepared fruit into a baking tray with a lip tall enough to keep in the liquid. Pour the flavoured wine over the fruit and roast, uncovered, until just soft. Check the plums after 15 to 20 minutes. The apples, if hard, may take up to 40 minutes. Remove any fruit that is soft and return the rest to the oven to continue cooking. Lay the cooked fruit out in a serving dish and leave to cool. Sieve and reserve the cooking liquid. To serve, gently warm the liquid and pour it into the dish to about halfway up he fruit; don't drown it, or the pudding will be over sweet. For the coconut cream, warm the coconut milk with the sugar and stir to dissolve. Mix the cornflour with a little water to make a paste and add. Stirring all the time, bring to the boil to thicken. Cool. Whip the cream until stiff. Whisk the coconut 'custard'. Mix a little custard into the cream to loosen it and then fold the two together.

<u>Variation:</u> Summer Berry Compote

Use any combination of berries you like. Cook blackcurrants, gooseberries and redcurrants gently with a very small amount of water until just beginning to produce juice. Sweeten to bring out the fruit flavour but not taste sweet and thicken with a little cornflour. Cool. Just before serving mix in fresh raspberries and or (chopped) strawberries.

Pear and Ginger Upside-down Pudding

We like to serve a hot pudding after the prawn buffet and this one with its vibrant mix of spices is perfect. It is important not to cut the silicon paper or else the butter and sugar will drip onto the floor of the oven.

serves 8

50g / 2oz butter
110g / 4oz soft brown sugar
2 to 3 pears peeled and sliced
85g / 3oz black treacle
110g / 4oz soft brown sugar
50g / 2oz butter
175g / 6oz self-raising flour
½ tsp bicarbonate of soda
2 tsp ground cinnamon
1 tsp ground ginger
¼ tsp ground nutmeg
1 egg
110ml / 4 fl oz milk

Without cutting the paper, line a 25cm / 10in round cake tin with silicon paper. You will need to pleat the paper along the sides. Preheat the oven to 180°C / gas mark 4. Melt the first butter and sugar together and spread in the base of the tin. Arrange the pears on this mixture. Gently melt the black treacle with the second lot of butter and sugar. Sift the flour, bicarb. and spices together. Beat together the egg and milk. Mix the melted ingredients into the dry and then stir in the liquid. Pour over the pears and bake for 35 to 40 minutes. Cool for a minute or so before turning out to serve with pouring cream or custard.

Figgy Crumble

During the winter we often get together to check out new recipes and inventions. Alan is not really a pudding person but he did have seconds when I tested this unusual crumble! Serve with custard or cream, or both.

Serves 6

110g / 4oz dried figs
110g / 4oz mixed dried fruit salad
water to not quite cover
50g / 2oz large, juicy raisins
280ml / ½ pint sweet sherry
175g / 6oz plain flour
85g / 3oz granulated sugar
85g / 3oz butter

Roughly chop the figs and larger pieces of dried fruit and put into a pan with the water. Bring these gently to the boil and simmer, covered, for 10 minutes. Add the raisins, cover, and continue to simmer for 15 more minutes. Remove from the heat, add the sherry, cover and leave to cool. Preheat the oven to 190°C / gas mark 5. Make the crumble mixture by rubbing the flour, sugar and butter together with your fingers, or whizzing them in a food processor, until they are like fine breadcrumbs. Transfer the fruit to an ovenproof dish. When ready to cook, spoon the crumble evenly on to the fruit and bake for 25 minutes. The top should be a nice brown colour and the fruit should be bubbling.

Hazelnut Shortcake

Here is something I first made 40 years ago and is just as good today. It comes from the Constance Spry Cookery book first published in 1956! I have quite a collection of old books and even in this age of endless recipes on the internet I still love looking through them; a huge source of information and inspiration.

Serves 8
85g / 3oz hazelnuts
pinch salt
60g / 2½ oz caster sugar
125g / 4½ oz plain flour
95g / 3½ oz butter
280ml / ½ pint double cream
2 tbs icing sugar
2 tbs liqueur of choice (optional)
4 fresh ripe peaches, or other seasonal fruit

Preheat the oven to 190°C / gas mark 5. Toast the hazels in the oven for 10 minutes, rub to remove the skins and grind. Put in a bowl with the sugar, flour and butter and rub together with the fingertips. Work into a soft dough and chill for 30 minutes. Preheat the oven to 180°C / gas mark 4. Line a flat baking tray with silicon paper. Roll the dough on the baking tray to a circle about 1.25cm / ½ in thick and crimp the edges. Bake for 20 minutes until starting to tinge brown. Cool slightly before lifting off the tray and finish cooling on a rack. Stone and slice the peaches. Whisk the cream with the icing sugar and liqueur until just holding its shape. Pile on top of the shortcake and top with the fruit.

Chocolate Roulade

This is a bit retro, but it is a classic and just so good. Light and not too sweet, we have tried variations but none come up to the original. You will need two clean tea towels.

serves 6 to 8
4 eggs, separated
110g / 4oz caster sugar
110g / 4oz dark (70%) chocolate
¾ tbs cocoa powder, sifted
200ml / 7 fl oz double cream, whipped

Preheat the oven to 180°C / gas mark 4. Line a 30x23cm / 12x9in traybake tin with silicon paper. Wet a tea towel and then squeeze it out as hard as you can. Melt the chocolate and cocoa over hot water. Whisk the yolks and 85g / 3oz of the sugar until very thick. Whisk the whites until very stiff and whisk in the rest of the sugar. Working quickly, combine the yolk mixture with the chocolate. Mix in about a quarter of the whites to loosen the mix then fold in the rest very gently. Turn into the prepared tin and bake for 20 minutes. Do not turn out. Place a clean dry tea towel over the sponge and the damp one on top and leave to cool. Turn out onto greaseproof paper sprinkled with castor sugar. Spread on the cream and roll up. Sprinkle with more sugar to serve.

Old-Fashioned Posset

This delightful traditional pudding is incredibly easy. If you have a rose-scented geranium, that unusual variation is well worth a try. The raspberry one is beyond perfect. When not being followed by a cheeseboard, we serve posset with petticoat shortbread (page159).

serves 6

400ml / 14 fl oz double cream
85g / 3oz caster sugar
zest 1 lemon
50ml / 2 fl oz lemon juice

Place the cream, sugar and zest in a pan and warm gently until the sugar is dissolved, Turn the heat up and, stirring all the time, boil hard for 2 and a half minutes. Remove from the heat, mix in the lemon juice and strain into ramekins or small glasses. Cover with a clean tea-towel and refrigerate for at least 4 hours or overnight. Decorate with edible flowers or crystallised lemon pieces.

Variation: Rose Posset

Use 5 leaves of rose-scented geranium instead of the lemon zest. It is lovely with fresh berries.

Variation: Raspberry Posset

Blend 200g / 7oz of raspberries with 3 tablespoons of dry white wine. Blend and sieve to remove the seeds. Cook 300ml / ½ pint double cream with 150g / 5oz sugar as above. Stir in the fruit and pour into ramekins. Decorate with a sprinkling of freeze dried raspberry powder or fresh raspberries.

Variation: Blackcurrant Posset

Cook 200g / 7oz of blackcurrants with 3 tablespoons of water until soft, cool and push through a sieve. Mix with 3 tablespoons of dry white wine and 2 teaspoons of lemon juice. Proceed as for the raspberry posset.

Cranachan

This classic very Scottish dessert is not an exact science and is all a matter of taste. Whisky, smoky or delicate; honey, strong heather or mild blossom; a light touch of oatmeal or more for a richer, heavier confection. The choice is with the maker. Have everything ready in advance but don't assemble until the last minute or the oatmeal will go soft and stodgy.

serves 8

560ml / 1 pint fresh double cream
4 to 6 tbs whisky
1 to 2 tbs runny honey
lots of fresh ripe raspberries
2 to 4 tbs pinhead oatmeal

Sieve the oatmeal to remove any dust or small bits. Toast it carefully in a heavy based pan over a medium heat so it takes on a little colour and a nutty flavour. Cool. Whisk the cream until just holding shape. Gently fold in the whisky and honey to taste. Reserve a few berries and oatmeal and fold the rest into the cream. Turn into a glass serving dish and sprinkle with the reserved berries and oatmeal.

Apricot Upside-down Pudding

One year we ended up with a 25 kilo sack of dried apricots by mistake and had to think of ways to use them. This was such a favourite that it continued long after the sack was gone. We then hit on using some dark un-sulphured apricots as an attractive colour contrast. These have a rich toffee flavour and are available in health food shops. We serve it hot with custard but cold, (and with double the sponge), it also makes an excellent traybake for packed lunches. You will need to allow time to soak the apricots.

serves 6
40g / 1½ oz butter
40g / 1½ oz dark soft brown sugar
dried apricots, orange and brown
85g / 3oz butter, softened
85g / 3oz light soft brown sugar
1 egg, beaten
some soaking liquid from the apricots
110g / 4oz self-raising flour

Take enough apricots to cover half the base of the tin. Now put them in a large bowl, well cover with boiling water, and leave to soak for at least 12 hours. Without cutting the paper, line a 23cm / 9in round cake tin with silicon paper. Do this by pleating the paper along the sides then cut off any points that are sticking up or they will burn. Preheat the oven to 180°C / gas mark 4. Melt the first amount of butter and sugar carefully, pour into the prepared tin and spread it out. Drain and cut the soaked apricots in half around their equator and place in a pattern on the mixture in the base. Beat the remaining butter and sugar until soft and fluffy. Beat in the egg and fold in the flour and enough of the soaking liquid to make a soft consistency. Spread this over the apricots and bake for about 30 minutes or until an inserted skewer comes out clean. Turn out and serve while still hot.

Lemon Sauce Pudding

A lovely old-fashioned recipe which we have often used when we have small numbers in the dining room. (It is a bit last minute-ish for when we are busy.) It is light and lemony with a sauce under the sponge.

serves 4
1 lemon, grated rind and juice
50g / 2oz butter, well softened
110g / 4oz caster sugar
2 eggs, separated
280ml / ½ pint milk
50g / 2oz self-raising flour

Have ready an 850ml / 1½ pint ovenproof dish and a bain-marie to fit. Preheat the oven to 200°C / gas mark 6. Beat the butter, lemon rind and sugar until light and fluffy. Add the egg yolks, lemon juice and flour, mix well then stir in the milk. Whisk the egg whites stiffly and fold in. Pour into the dish and put in the bain-marie with cold water ½ way up the dish. Bake for about 45 minutes until the top is set and spongy to the touch.

Hazelnut Chocolate Pear Torte

This is a gorgeous chocolate pudding from Chloe, who cooked with us for the 2015 season, and loves chocolate as much as I do! It looks spectacular for a special occasion.

serves 8 to10

4 eggs, separated
125g / 4½ oz sugar
125g / 4½ oz dark (70%) chocolate
125g / 4½ oz butter
125g / 4½ oz hazelnuts
4 pears

Line a 28cm / 11in cake or tart tin with one piece of uncut silicon paper and snip off any corners. Preheat the oven to 190°C / gas mark 5. Roast the hazelnuts for 10 minutes, rub off the skins and process until finely ground. Reduce the oven temperature to to 180°C / gas mark 4. Peel the pears, cut into thirds and scoop out the cores. Melt the chocolate and butter over hot water. Whisk the egg yolks and sugar until light and fluffy. Whisk the egg whites until stiff. Carefully fold everything except the pears together and spread into the tin. Gently place the pears on top and bake for 30 to 40 minutes until just set. Cool in the tin. To serve, warm very slightly, turn upside-down on a board, remove the paper and invert onto a platter. Sprinkle lightly with icing sugar and serve with pouring cream.

Tiramisu

When chilled, this should be solid enough to cut into pieces for serving. Vin santo, Tia Maria, or brandy can be substituted for the amaretto, and sponge fingers (more Italian, less Dounie!) for the home-made sponge.

serves 6

a 2 egg trifle sponge
450g / 1lb mascarpone cheese
4 egg yolks
70g / 2½ oz icing sugar
2 tbs amaretto
175ml / 6 fl oz strong black coffee
2 tbs amaretto
cocoa powder or dark chocolate

Find a flat serving dish approximately 5cm / 2in deep which holds at least 1.42 litres / 2½ pints. Square or oblong is easiest but not essential. Make the trifle sponge as in the sherry trifle recipe on page 81. Beat the mascarpone until soft. Whisk together the yolks, icing sugar and first lot of amaretto until thick and creamy. Add this slowly to the mascarpone making sure there are no lumps. Mix the coffee with the second lot of amaretto. Cut the sponge into pieces. Layer up in the serving dish thus: mixture, sponge (dipped lightly and speedily into the coffee and amaretto mix), mixture, dipped sponge, mixture. Chill for as long as possible and decorate with sieved cocoa powder or grated chocolate.

Malva Pudding

Martin and Jane brought this recipe back from a trip to South Africa where it is quite a tradition. Although it seems to be a sticky toffee pudding on steroids it is remarkably light and easy to eat.

serves 8

1 tin apricots (411g), drained
25g / 1 oz butter
125g / 4½ fl oz milk
200g / 7 oz sugar
2 large eggs
1 tbs apricot jam
175g / 6 oz self-raising flour
1 tsp bicarbonate of soda
good pinch salt
1 tsp vinegar
<u>for the sauce:</u>
125ml / 4½ fl oz double cream
60g / 2½ oz unsalted butter
60g / 2½ oz soft brown sugar
60ml / 2½ fl oz orange juice

Choose a 1.85 litre / 3¼ pint ovenproof dish. Halve the apricots and place in a layer in the dish. Preheat the oven to 180°C / gas mark 4. Melt the butter with the milk and cool slightly. Whisk the sugar and eggs until light and thick and whisk in the jam. Sift the flour, bicarbonate of soda and salt together. Whisk the melted mixture into the eggs and sugar and add the vinegar. Gently fold in the flour and pour the batter over the apricots. Bake for 45 to 50 minutes, covering lightly with foil after 20 minutes to avoid over browning. Melt the sauce ingredients together. Prick the cooked pudding all over and pour the sauce over the top. Serve with pouring cream or custard.

<u>Variation:</u>

Raspberry Malva Pudding

Substitute the apricot jam and fruit with raspberry jam and 8oz raspberries. Use water in the sauce instead of orange juice.

Chocolate and Blackcurrant Pots

This is another recipe from Chloe. It combines two of our favourite ingredients; dark chocolate and blackcurrants from the garden. You can use fresh or frozen fruit, but add a few more minutes cooking time for the frozen.

serves 8

110g / 4oz dark (70%) chocolate
110g / 4oz butter
2 eggs and 2 extra yolks
110g / 4oz plain flour
50g / 2oz maple syrup
50g / 2oz golden syrup
8 tbs blackcurrants

Butter 8 ramekin dishes. Preheat the oven to 180°C / gas mark 4. Melt the chocolate and butter over water. Whisk the eggs and yolks for 10 to 12 minutes until very thick. Fold everything together and pour into the ramekins. Bake for 15 to 20 minutes or until set.

cheesecakes

Chocolate Cheesecake

You can increase or decrease the amount of cocoa to get the level of chocolate that you like. Whatever you decide, the chocolate is enhanced by the rich dairy content making it velvety and scrumptious.

Serves 12
225g / 8oz dark (70%) chocolate
225g / 8oz cream cheese
4 dsp cocoa
1 tin (397g) sweetened condensed milk
430ml / ¾ pint double cream
chocolate curls
for the base:
70g / 2½ oz butter
270g / 9½ oz chocolate digestive biscuits

Choose a straight sided dish, clip tin, or loose-bottomed cake tin about 20cm / 8in diameter and line it with cling film. Melt the chocolate in a bowl over hot (not boiling) water. Once melted, cool slightly. In another bowl, whisk the cream cheese, cocoa, condensed milk and cream together until smooth. Add the chocolate and whisk again until well mixed and starting to thicken. Spoon into the tin and push down so it fills the shape of the tin without any air gaps. Melt the butter and cool slightly. Crush the biscuits as finely as you can and stir in the butter. Spoon this evenly over the chocolate mixture and smooth the top, pressing lightly. Fold the excess cling film over the top and refrigerate. To serve, fold back the cling film, turn out onto a plate and carefully remove the cling film. Sprinkle with chocolate curls, (white chocolate makes a great contrast).

Variation:

Mocha Cheesecake

Substitute half of the cocoa with barista style instant coffee powder.

Baked Vanilla Cheesecake

This is lighter than many recipes. It is really versatile and if you want to serve a topping or fruit sauce with it, all kinds work well.

serves 6

110g / 4oz digestive biscuits
40g / 1½ oz butter
300g cream cheese
75g caster sugar
2 eggs
1 egg yolk
½ tsp vanilla extract
1 tbs lemon juice
zest ½ lemon
140ml / 5 fl oz sour cream
1 tbs caster sugar
1 tsp vanilla extract

Line a 15cm / 6in clip or loose based tin with silicon paper. Use a double layer of strong foil to create a cover for the outside of the tin to make it waterproof. Find a tin suitable for a bain-marie. Crush the biscuits and melt the butter. Mix together and press into the tin. Preheat the oven to 190°C / gas mark 5. Beat the cream cheese until smooth and beat in the sugar, eggs and egg yolk. Add the vanilla and lemon zest and juice. Pour into the tin and place in the bain-marie with boiling water to halfway up the sides. Bake for about 30 minutes. It should feel set but not rigidly so. Mix the sour cream, sugar and vanilla and pour over the cheesecake. Return to the oven for a further 15 minutes. Remove from the oven and the bain-marie to cool then chill in the fridge. Unmould and serve with your chosen topping.

Variation:

Baked Lemon Cheesecake

Use the zest and juice of 2 lemons and just a few drops of vanilla. The sour cream topping is the same.

White Chocolate Cheesecake

Jamie used to serve this on Eda Frandsen and passed the recipe on to the Doune kitchen. Quick and easy, it is best made in a dish as it is rather soft to turn out. Be very sparing with any topping as it will mask the delicate flavour; we prefer a very light squiggle of dark chocolate.

serves 4 to 6

110g / 4oz digestive biscuits
50g / 2oz butter
110g / 4oz white chocolate
225g / 8oz mascarpone
70ml / 2½ fl oz double cream
juice ½ lemon

Choose a small, shallow serving dish. Crush the biscuits and melt the butter. Mix together, and press lightly into the dish. Melt the chocolate over hot (not boiling) water. In a bowl, mix the lemon and mascarpone until smooth and add the cream bit by bit. Add the chocolate and fold all together evenly. Spread onto the base and chill.

Toffee Cheesecake

The simplest cheesecake of all, this came from the original Cranks cookery book. We have increased the amount of muscovado to get a good toffee flavour, but the original was the lemon version below. You could do any proportion in between according to taste.

Serves 6

110g / 4oz dark muscovado sugar
juice ½ lemon
225g / 8oz cream cheese
110ml / 4 fl oz double cream, whipped
175g / 6oz digestive biscuits
85g / 3oz butter, melted
a little melted chocolate to decorate

Choose a tin or dish, any shape but with straight sides, about 15cm / 6in diameter or equivalent and line it with cling film. Mix the sugar with the lemon juice until smooth and beat in the cream cheese. Fold in the cream and spread into the dish. Crush the biscuits and mix with the butter. Spread evenly on top of the filling and refrigerate. To serve, turn out, remove the cling film and drizzle with chocolate.

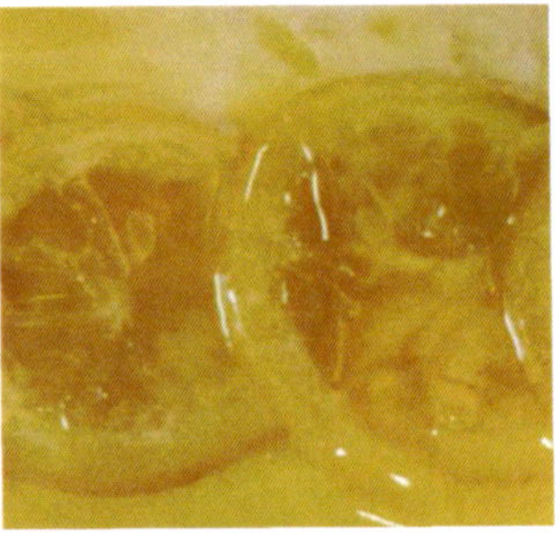

Variation: Lemon Cheesecake

Use just 50g / 2oz muscovado sugar and add the zest of a lemon. Instead of chocolate use any fresh fruit to decorate with a glaze if you like. Raspberries, strawberries or poached lemon slices are all great.

Ginger and Rhubarb Cheesecake

Brought to us by Iain who cooked with us in 2016. The subtle ginger flavour along with the spice in the base make an unusual twist. It is simpler than it looks!

serves 5 to 6

for the fruit:

350g / 12oz fresh rhubarb
½ tbs demerara sugar
juice ½ lemon
¼ cup water
½ cup sugar
½ tbs stem ginger with syrup, chopped

for the filling:

110g / 4oz white chocolate
110g / 4oz cream cheese
110g / 4oz double cream, whipped
25g / 1oz stem ginger, finely chopped

for the base:

110g / 4oz digestives (or ginger nuts)
50g / 2oz butter, melted
½ tsp mixed spice (not of using ginger nuts)

Choose a tin or dish, any shape but with straight sides, about 15cm / 6in diameter or equivalent and line it with cling film. Preheat the oven to 170°C / gas mark 3. Cut the rhubarb to the size required to make a pattern on the base of your dish. Place the cut fruit on a baking tray and sprinkle with the demerara sugar and lemon. Open roast for 20 to 30 minutes until soft but not collapsing. Allow to cool. Arrange the fruit on the base of the dish. Put the water into the baking tray and stir to collect any remaining juice and dislodge any bits of fruit. Pour this into a small pan and add the sugar and stem ginger. Boil together until syrupy and leave to cool. Melt the chocolate over hot (not boiling) water, cool a little and mix in the cream cheese, beating well so that it is smooth. Fold in the whipped cream and finely chopped ginger. Spoon the filling on top of the fruit and smooth over, pushing down to remove any air bubbles. Crush the biscuits very finely and mix with the butter and spices if using. When cool, spread evenly on top of the filling. Refrigerate. To serve, turn out, remove the cling film and strain the syrup over the fruit to make a glaze.

Variation: **Ginger and Pear Cheesecake**

Use 3 fresh pears, peeled, sliced in 6's and roasted, instead of the rhubarb.

ice creams

We don't use an ice cream maker and develop all our ice cream recipes to be made without constant attention through the freezing process. For serving direct from the freezer, we often use a fluted flan dish.

Christmas Ice Cream

The basis of this recipe was given to us by a guest who always serves it instead of Christmas pudding. It is great at any time of year but we still decorate it with holly! Remember to soak the fruit the day before.

serves 6

40g / 1½ oz no-soak apricots
40g / 1½ oz no-soak pitted prunes
40g / 1½ oz raisins
40g / 1½ oz sultanas
40g / 1½ oz cranberries
3 tbs brandy
210ml / 7½ fl oz double cream
2 eggs, separated
1 tbs caster sugar

Chop the apricots and prunes and soak all the fruit in the brandy overnight. Put a shallow 850ml / 1½ pint freezer proof serving dish into the fridge to cool. Whisk the egg yolks with half the sugar until thick and creamy. Whip the cream until stiff. Whisk the egg whites until stiff and whip in the rest of the sugar to stabilise the foam. Mix the fruit, egg yolk mixture and cream well together. Fold in the egg whites and pour into the chilled dish. Freeze. Take out about 15 minutes before serving to allow it to soften.

Rhubarb Ice Cream

Simple and delicious, one of the most seductive ways to serve rhubarb.

serves 8

500g / 18oz prepared rhubarb
250g / 9oz sugar
156ml / 5½ fl oz double cream
2 eggs, separated
1 dsp sugar

Carefully cook the rhubarb and sugar without water until soft. Cool. Put a shallow 1.14 litre / 2 pint freezer-proof serving dish into the fridge to cool. Blend the rhubarb until smooth. Whip the cream so it is stiff and mix in the egg yolks thoroughly. Add the rhubarb and combine well. Whisk the egg whites until stiff and whisk in the desert spoon of sugar. Fold about a quarter of the meringue thoroughly into the fruit mixture and then, very gently and carefully, fold in the rest. Pour into the chilled serving dish and freeze. Take out a good 15 minutes before serving.

St. Clements Ice Cream

Toppi introduced us to this delicious and wonderfully easy ice cream which has remained a firm favourite for 20 years.

serves 10
3 eggs
175g / 6oz caster sugar
280ml / ½ pint double cream
1 orange, zest and juice
1 lemon, zest and juice

Put a shallow 1.14 litre / 2 pint freezer-proof serving dish into the fridge to cool. Set aside 1 tablespoon of the sugar. Whisk the yolks and zest with the rest of the sugar until thick and creamy, then, still whisking, gradually add the lemon juice. It must still be thick so keep back some of the juice if it is getting too thin. Whisk the cream so it is stiff and fold in the orange juice and any remaining lemon juice. Blend a little of the yolk mixture into the cream until smooth and then mix in the rest. Whisk the egg whites until stiff and whisk in the tablespoon of sugar. Fold about a quarter of the meringue thoroughly into the cream mixture and then, very gently and carefully, fold in the rest. Pour into the chilled serving dish and freeze.

Variation:

Blackcurrant Ice Cream

Cook 225g / 8oz blackcurrants with 110ml / 4 fl oz water for 5 minutes. Sieve, discard the pulp and use the extract instead of the orange and lemon.

Strawberry and Redcurrant Ripple Ice Cream

Layering is the best method I have found for getting plenty of ripple into the mix plus a pretty ripple effect on top. You need to start this recipe the day before eating.

serves 6
375g / 13oz strawberries
85g / 3oz sugar
juice 1 large orange
280ml / ½ pint double cream
more strawberries to serve
For the ripple:
3 tbs water
70g / 2½ oz sugar
70g / 2½ oz redcurrants

The day before, blend the strawberries, sugar and orange juice and place in a container in the freezer. Make the ripple by boiling the water and sugar together for 1 minute, adding the redcurrants and cooking until they have all burst. Strain through a sieve but do not press or the syrup will be cloudy. Cool. The next day, put a shallow 850ml / 1½ pint freezer-proof serving dish into the fridge to cool. Tip the frozen fruit mixture into a food processor and blend again. Whisk the cream and fold into the fruit. Put a layer of ice cream into the chilled dish, drizzle some of the redcurrant syrup on top and swirl briefly making a ripple effect. Repeat the process one or two times. Freeze. Remove from the freezer 15 minutes before serving with extra fresh strawberries.

Nougat Ice Cream

An unusual ice cream based on Italian meringue. Freshly made candied peel gives a zingy flavour and bright colour but you can use one tablespoon of bought peel if you don't have time. The ice cream stands alone but is also wonderful with hot chocolate sauce.

serves 8

1 large orange, peel only
2 tbs sugar
50g / 2oz flaked almonds
50g / 2oz raw pistachio nuts
50g / 2oz runny honey
110g / 4oz caster sugar
2 egg whites
280ml / ½ pint double cream
1 tsp vanilla extract

For the candied peel: Chop the orange peel finely. Heat the sugar in 4 tablespoons of water, add the peel and cook gently for about half an hour. There should only be a little liquid left. (Keep an eye in case it dries and burns, add a little more water if needed). Rinse with water and drain. Put a shallow 1.14 litre / 2 pint freezer-proof serving dish into the fridge to cool. Toast all the nuts then chop the pistachios roughly. Measure the honey, sugar and 3 tablespoons of water into a pan and heat gently to dissolve the sugar. Increase the heat and boil for 1 minute until syrupy. Allow to cool slightly. Whisk the egg whites until stiff, then, whisking all the time, add the honey syrup in a steady, thin, stream. When all the syrup has been added, continue whisking for a few minutes until the meringue is thick and glossy. Whip the double cream with the vanilla. Reserve a few nuts and peel for decoration. Fold everything else together and pour into the chilled serving dish. Sprinkle with the reserved nuts and peel and freeze. It doesn't go really hard so there is no need to bring it out of the freezer early.

Cardamom Ice Cream

This is a subtle and sophisticated ice cream.

serves 8

1 tsp cardamom seeds
140ml / ¼ pint milk
140ml / ¼ pint double cream
1 tsp cornflour
3 eggs, separated
95g / 3½ oz sugar
280ml / ½ pint double cream, whipped
a little melted dark chocolate

Crush the seeds slightly, put in a pan with the milk and cream and heat until bubbles start to appear at the edge of the pan. Turn off the heat and leave to infuse for at least 1 hour. Blend in the cornflour and bring to the boil, stirring, to thicken very slightly. Whisk the egg yolks and 85g / 3oz of the sugar together, strain the creamy milk onto it and whisk again. Return to a clean pan and cook gently, stirring constantly, until the mixture coats the back of the spoon. Cover and leave to cool. Put a shallow 1.14 litre / 2 pint freezer-proof serving dish into the fridge to cool. Mix a little of the cooled custard into the whipped cream and blend, then add the rest. Whisk the egg whites to peaks and whisk in the remaining 10g / ½ oz of sugar. Gently fold this into the cream mixture half at a time. Pour into the chilled dish, cover with cling film and freeze. Remove from the freezer 10 minutes before eating and decorate with a thin stream of melted chocolate in squiggles.

Variation:

Fresh Peppermint Ice Cream

Instead of the cardamom, use 6 good stalks of fresh peppermint. It is best left overnight to infuse properly.

White Chocolate and Baileys Ice Cream

This lovely rich recipe came from Kristy.

serves 10

280ml / ½ pint milk
1 tsp cornflour
3 eggs, separated
50g / 2oz sugar
280ml / ½ pint double cream
140ml / 5 fl oz Baileys Irish Cream
150g / 6oz white chocolate
a little milk chocolate to decorate

Blend the milk and cornflour and, stirring constantly, bring to the boil to thicken very slightly. Reserve one tablespoon of sugar. Whisk the egg yolks with the rest of the sugar. Still whisking, pour the milk onto it. Return to the pan and cook gently, stirring constantly, until the mixture coats the back of the spoon. Cover and leave to cool. Put a shallow 1.14 litre / 2 pint freezer-proof serving dish into the fridge to cool. Melt the chocolate over hot (not boiling) water. Whisk the cream with the Baileys until thick. Blend a little of the cream into the cooled custard and then mix in the rest, followed by the chocolate. Whisk the egg whites to peaks and whisk in the remaining sugar. Fold about a quarter of the meringue thoroughly into the cream mixture and then very gently and carefully fold in the rest. Pour into the chilled dish and freeze. Remove from the freezer 10 minutes before serving and drizzle with the chocolate.

pavlovas

We started doing Pavlovas the first year of the restaurant and they have become a bit of a tradition ever since. It is an unusual week if we don't serve one. I find it hard to believe that to start with we used Mary's old (distinctly sad) 'bedspring coil whisk'. An electric hand whisk was a revelation!

Almond Praline Pavlova

I came up with this when I wanted another choice to fill the gap when there is no suitable fresh fruit around. Use the best quality almond extract you can find.

serves 6
3 egg whites
175g / 6oz granulated sugar
1 tsp cornflour, sifted
1 tsp vinegar
2 tbs flaked almonds (optional)
50g / 2oz caster sugar
50g / 2oz whole almonds
280ml / ½ pint double cream
¼ tsp almond extract
2 tbs brandy
25g / 1oz dark chocolate, melted

Whisk the egg whites until very firm. Gradually add the sugar, whisking after each addition. Keep whisking until smooth and shiny. Fold in the cornflour and vinegar. Preheat the oven to 150°C / gas mark 2. Line a baking tray with silicon paper. Spread the mixture in a circle about 150cm / 6in diameter. Run the back of a spoon firmly up the sides of the meringue making vertical furrows all the way around. If you want, sprinkle with the flaked almonds especially up the sides. Bake for 50 minutes. It will rise and spread a bit and should be very slightly coloured. After baking, turn off the heat and leave to cool in the oven with the door closed. To make the praline, line a small baking tray with silicon paper. Put the sugar and almonds in a heavy-based saucepan to evenly cover the base. Heat gently, without stirring, until the sugar has melted and turned golden. Swirl the melted sugar gently to coat the almonds and pour immediately onto the tin. Leave to cool. Break the praline up and crush so it is nice and fine. Keep in an airtight container if you are not using immediately. Lift the meringue on to a serving plate. Whisk the cream with the almond extract and brandy until just holding shape and stir in most of the crushed praline. Pile onto the meringue and spread out roughly. Decorate with the chocolate and sprinkle with the last of the praline.

Lemon Curd and Fresh Fruit Pavlova

I love doing fresh fruit Pavlovas, they are so beautiful. We can muster fresh Doune grown fruit for much of the summer plus we freeze some for purées out of season.

serves 6

3 egg whites
175g / 6oz granulated sugar
1 tsp cornflour, sifted
1 tsp vinegar
280ml / ½ pint double cream, lightly whipped
3 tbs homemade lemon curd (page128)
lots of fresh fruit in season

Whisk the egg whites until very firm. Gradually add the sugar, whisking after each addition. Keep whisking until smooth and shiny. Fold in the cornflour and vinegar. Preheat the oven to 150°C / gas mark 2. Line a baking tray with silicon paper. Spread the mixture in a circle about 150cm / 6in diameter. Run the back of a spoon firmly up the sides of the meringue making vertical furrows all the way around. Bake for 50 minutes. It will rise and spread a bit and should be very slightly coloured. After baking, turn off the heat and leave to cool in the oven with the door closed. When crisp, lift on to a serving plate. Spread with the cream, place on teaspoonfuls of lemon curd and swirl this in very lightly. Arrange the fruit on top.

Variation:

Apple and Bramble Pavlova

Omit the lemon curd. Cook 2 to 3 cooking apples and sweeten very sparingly, purée and cool. Bring 175g / 6oz of brambles slowly to the boil (no water) and simmer for 10 minutes to extract all the juice. Sweeten just enough to bring out the flavour, strain, thicken slightly with cornflour and cool. Spread the apple onto the meringue, pour on the bramble juice and swirl lightly. Spread with cream and top with fresh apple slices and a few choice fresh brambles.

Variation:

Blackcurrant Pavlova

Omit the lemon curd. Cook 225g / 8oz blackcurrants with very little water until just starting to pop. Add sugar to bring out the flavour of the fruit without sweetening, thicken slightly with cornflour and cool. Spoon directly onto the pavlova and top with cream. Decorate with fresh berries and blackcurrant leaves.

Variation:

Rhubarb and Strawberry Pavlova

Omit the lemon curd. Cook 350g rhubarb gently without water until soft. Purée, sweeten to bring out the flavour and cool. Add 110g / 4oz chopped strawberries. Spoon directly onto the pavlova and top with cream. Decorate with more fresh strawberries.

Nougatine Pavlova

Unusual, chewy and delicious, this has been with us right from the start. You can also crush the baked meringue, fold it into whipped cream or softened vanilla ice cream and freeze in a cling film lined loaf tin. Turn it out and slice to serve. For the sauce, we cook redcurrants and blackcurrants until soft and press through a sieve. Sweeten just enough to bring out the flavour.

serves 6
70g / 2½ oz walnuts
70g / 2½ oz dates
70g / 2½ oz digestive biscuits
3 egg whites
175g / 6oz granulated sugar
280ml / ½ pint double cream
sharp fruit sauce to serve

Chop the walnuts and dates quite small and crush the biscuits to make fine crumbs. Preheat the oven to 150°C / gas mark 2. Line a baking tray with silicon paper. Whisk the egg whites until very firm. Gradually add the sugar, whisking after each addition. Keep whisking until smooth and shiny. Fold in the nuts, dates and biscuits and spread the mixture on the tray in a circle about 20cm / 8in diameter. Bake for 40 minutes. It will spread a bit and should be very slightly coloured. After baking, turn off the heat and leave to cool in the oven with the door closed. When crisp, lift on to a serving plate. Whip the cream lightly and spread onto the meringue. Drizzle with a little sauce and serve the rest in a jug.

Walnut Tart

This was Ann-Marie's favourite pudding and I can't make it without thinking of her.

serves 8 to 10
26cm / 10in blind baked shortcrust pastry tart shell
175g / 6oz walnuts
110g / 4oz butter
275g / 10oz castor sugar
2 tsp ground cinnamon
2 eggs, beaten

Preheat the oven to 180°C / gas mark 4. Cover the baked base with walnuts. Melt the butter, sugar and cinnamon slowly together then cool slightly. Beat in the eggs and pour the mixture over the walnuts. Bake for 25 minutes. Leave to cool for 15 minutes before removing from the tin. Serve warm with lightly whipped cream.

tarts

We have a wide selection of tart recipes and depending on what other puddings are planned for a week I will almost always include one. Quantities given are for a 26cm / 10in shallow loose-bottomed tart tin which is quite a big tart serving 8 to 10. A 22cm / 8½ in tin will serve 6 and will take two thirds of the pastry and filling. We use our rich shortcrust pastry (page 161) but your own recipe or bought is fine. Pastry made with 175g / 6oz of flour will just fit the large tin but must be thinly rolled. If you want a touch more leeway you will need to make a bit more.

Syrup and Apple Tart

There is always a temptation to put lemon zest in a syrup tart but I think it overpowers the flavour of the syrup. The right amount of apple, however, works really well.

serves 8 to 10

26cm / 10in blind baked shortcrust pastry tart shell
600g / 1lb 5oz golden syrup
150g / 5oz fresh white breadcrumbs
2 large or 3 small Bramley apples

Cook the peeled, cored and sliced apples with a little water until very soft and mash or blend so there are no lumps. Weigh the purée; you need 400g / 14oz. Preheat the oven to 180°C / gas mark 4. Warm the syrup and mix in the breadcrumbs and purée then pour into the pastry case. Bake for about 30 minutes until just set. Serve warm with pouring cream or custard

Apple and Almond Tart

A really easy and very beautiful version of French apple tart.

serves 8 to 10

26cm / 10in blind baked shortcrust pastry tart shell
225g / 8oz marzipan
700g / 1½ lb cooking apples
sugar to taste
3 red eating apples
3 dsp redcurrant jelly

Peel and core the cooking apples, cook gently to a pulp and sweeten to taste. Preheat the oven to 180°C / gas mark 4. Roll the marzipan to fit and place in the base of the tart. Fill the tart with the apple purée. Core the eating apples, slice thinly and arrange on top. Bake for 20 to 30 mins until the apples are starting to soften. Gently heat the jelly and brush on to the apple slices to glaze. Serve warm or cold with pouring cream.

Prune and Brandy Tart

This rich, ambrosial filling is from a Skye Gyngell recipe. Fragrant and so unusual, it could just possibly be my favourite of all the tarts...

serves 8 to 10

26cm / 10in blind baked shortcrust pastry tart shell
225g / 8oz stoned prunes
35g / 1¼ oz unsalted butter
3 eggs, beaten
150g / 5oz caster sugar
3 drops vanilla extract
1 tsp orange flower water
6 tbs double cream
4 tbs ground almonds
4 tbs brandy

Preheat the oven to 180°C / gas mark 4. Halve the prunes and soak in boiling water for 10 minutes. Remove and drain. Melt the butter and allow to cool slightly. In a large bowl combine the eggs, sugar, vanilla, orange flower water, cream and almonds until evenly blended then stir in the butter. Scatter the prunes evenly over the base and pour the mixture over the top. Bake for 25 minutes until just set. Remove from the oven and drizzle with the brandy avoiding wetting the pastry. Allow to cool for 15 minutes before removing from the tin. Serve warm with pouring cream.

Variation:

Apple and Calvados Tart

Instead of the prunes, peel, core and thickly slice 4 eating apples. Fry them gently in 25g / 1oz butter until starting to soften. Sprinkle over 25g / 1oz granulated sugar, cook to caramelise to a lovely brown and cool. Omit the orange flower water and use Calvados instead of brandy.

Chocolate Tart

Martina, who was with us for the 2007 season, is well remembered for her enthusiastic love of two things; dolphins and this rich and gooey chocolate tart which came courtesy of Martin's sister Emma.

serves 8 to 10

26cm / 10in blind baked shortcrust pastry tart shell
175g / 5oz butter, unsalted
175g / 5oz dark (70%) chocolate
1 tbs cocoa powder
2 tbs golden syrup
2 eggs, beaten
175g / 5oz caster sugar
1 tsp vanilla extract

Preheat the oven to 180°C / gas mark 4. Melt the butter, chocolate, cocoa and golden syrup over hot water. Whisk the eggs, sugar and vanilla until thick and mousse-like. Whisk the two mixtures together and pour into the tart case. Bake for 25 minutes until just set. If serving straight away leave to cool for 15 minutes before removing from the tin. If reheating, 10 minutes in a moderate oven will warm it through. Serve with pouring cream and a light dusting of icing sugar over the tart.

.Lemon Tart

Any tart with a filling that is runny to start with has the potential for a (to coin a phrase) 'soggy bottom' but if you follow the instructions below you should win the battle. It is important to bake the pastry so that it is really crisp in the first place and to fill any cracks that have appeared in the pastry or else the filling will just run out!

serves 8 to 10
26cm / 10in blind baked sweet shortcrust pastry tart shell
4 eggs
4 lemons, zest and juice
175g / 6oz caster sugar
160ml / 5½ fl oz double cream

Arrange the oven so that the tart will go in the middle and there are no racks above it. This should allow you to pour the filling into the tart in the oven so avoiding having to move the tart with runny filling. Preheat the oven to 190°C / gas mark 5. Separate one of the eggs and reserve the white. Whisk all the remaining ingredients together (including the yolk) until smooth but not fluffy and transfer to a jug. Break the reserved egg white up a little with a fork and brush it liberally over the surface of the cooked pastry case. Place the tart on a baking tray in the oven and bake for a few minutes until the pastry is hot. (Keep a careful eye to avoid burning.) Turn the oven down to 150°C / gas mark 2. Pour the filling into the hot pastry and bake for 20 to 30 minutes until just set. Try not to overdo it or the filling will develop cracks. Cool slightly before removing from the tin. Decorate with sifted icing sugar and serve warm with pouring cream.

Blackcurrant Tart

A basic frangipane tart. The sharpness of the blackcurrants is just perfect but don't be tempted to add extra or the tart will be too sour.

serves 8 to 10
26cm / 10in blind baked shortcrust pastry tart shell
175g / 6oz butter
175 / 6oz sugar
175g / 6oz ground almonds
3 eggs, beaten
175g / 6oz blackcurrants

Preheat the oven to 180°C / gas mark 4. Gently melt the butter and sugar, cool a little and beat in the almonds and eggs. Place the blackcurrants evenly on the pastry and pour the almond mixture over. Bake for 20 minutes until it is just starting to brown. (Add an extra 10 minutes if you are using frozen berries.) Serve warm or cold with pouring cream.

Variation: Raspberry Tart

Substituting raspberries for the blackcurrants makes a sweeter but still delicious tart.

Variation: Apple Tart

Prepare 3 apples as for the apple version of the Prune and Brandy tart. Pour the frangipane into the base and arrange the apples on top.

sorbets

When we serve a cheeseboard we need a small light sweet course so that people can do justice to the cheese, and sorbet fits the bill perfectly.

Each sorbet makes about 8 to 10 servings at 2 scoops each

Our general method: Boil sugar and water for 10 minutes to make a syrup and cool it. Produce a strained fruit extract, purée or juice. Freeze these together overnight. Either mash with a potato masher or blend in a food processor to make a smooth 'mash'. (If this is very mushy it is best to re-freeze it for an hour or so before the next step.) Fold in whipped egg white stabilised with a little sugar and refreeze. When serving, sorbets usually take about 5 minutes out of the freezer before you can scoop them. Our favourite decoration is a scattering of edible flowers.

Mint Chocolate Sorbet

75g / 2½ oz sugar
75ml 2½ fl oz water
150g / 5oz dark (70%) chocolate
2 tbs mint liqueur
280ml / ½ pint water
2 egg whites
1 tbs caster sugar

Dissolve the sugar in the first lot of water and bring to the boil. Remove from the heat and whisk in the chocolate until it is melted and smooth. Cool slightly, add the liqueur and second lot of water and mix well. Freeze and continue as our general method. A food processor or blender is best for this as it can be quite grainy if the ice crystals are not broken up really well. This does freeze quite hard so allow 5 to 10 minutes for it to be scoop-able.

Apple, Gin and Elderflower Sorbet

An idea I have been thinking about for many years but couldn't get right. Suzanne, who cooked with us for the 2017 season added the gin, and it was just what it needed.

200ml / 7 fl oz water
85g / 3oz sugar
580g / 1lb 4oz apple purée
2½ tbs elderflower cordial
50ml / 2 fl oz gin
2 egg whites
1 tbs caster sugar

Use our general method. You shouldn't need to sweeten the apple unless it is very sharp. Mix the cordial and gin into the purée and syrup before freezing. This doesn't freeze really hard and can usually be served straight from the freezer.

Gooseberry and Elderflower sorbet

560ml / 1 pint water
225g / 8oz sugar
450g / 1lb gooseberries
1 tbs elderflower cordial
2 egg whites
1 tbs caster sugar

Use our general method. Cook the gooseberries gently without water until soft, blend with the cordial and use as a purée.

Blackcurrant Sorbet

560ml / 1 pint water
225g / 8oz sugar
1lb blackcurrants + 2 tbs water
3 egg whites
1½ tbs caster sugar

Use our general method. Cook the blackcurrants gently with the 2 tbs of water until soft and push through a sieve to make the purée.

Mojito Sorbet

560ml / 1 pint water
225g / 8oz sugar
2 sprigs fresh sweet mint
zest and juice 4 limes
2 measures white rum
1 tbs fresh sweet mint, chopped fine

Use our general method. Include the zest and mint sprigs when making the syrup. Squeeze it well when you strain it, and add the juice, rum and chopped mint.

Ginger and Lime Sorbet

Martin's favourite sorbet and, if he was allowed, the only one we would ever serve! Be as accurate as you can with the ginger as the flavours are finely balanced.

560ml / 1 pint water
225g / 8oz sugar
25g / 1oz peeled fresh root ginger, sliced
zest and juice 4 limes
2 egg whites
1 tbs caster sugar

Use our general method. Include the zest and ginger when making the syrup. Squeeze it well when you strain it, and add the juice.

Bubbles and Pink Grapefruit Sorbet

150ml / 5 fl oz water
150g / 5oz sugar
250ml / 8½ fl oz pink grapefruit juice
200ml / 7 fl oz Cava or Prosecco
2 egg whites
1 tbs caster sugar

Use our general method. Use freshly squeezed grapefruit juice or from a carton. 200ml bottles of Cava or Prosecco are available. It will be soft enough to serve straight from the freezer.

Cheeseboard

Some years ago I attended a short cheesemaking course at a beautiful artisan dairy near Kyle of Lochalsh. This was really for my own interest and I didn't actually expect to come back and make cheese! However, our cheeseboards now include a variety of cheeses from the Doune kitchen. As ever, a selection of our home-made crackers and oatcakes and our own chutney or relish complement the cheeses.

crackers and oatcakes

Mary's Oatcakes

Our original oatcakes, still made every week of the season. They are crisp and hard and unlike any bought variety. The dough must be really sticky or it dries out too quickly and becomes difficult to handle. These go brilliantly with all cheese and also our home-made lemon curd (page128).

350g / 8oz medium oatmeal
½ tsp salt
14g / ½ oz butter, melted
boiling water

Preheat the oven to 170°C / gas mark 3. You will need two baking trays. Mix the oatmeal and salt. Pour in the butter and enough water to make a very soft, sticky, dough. With oatmeal on the work surface, roll into a long sausage and cut into discs. Squash each one, but don't make them too thin, and place on the trays. Bake both trays together for about an hour, swapping halfway, Turn the oatcakes over and continue for about 10 more minutes until well dried out and crisp. Cool on a wire rack.

Crispy Oatcakes

Due to the faster cooking time, these oatcakes have a light and tender texture. They came via Kathryn who was with us for the 2010 season. This recipe lends itself well to lots of variations.

350g / 8oz medium oatmeal
½ tsp salt
½ tsp sugar
½ tsp baking powder
75ml / 2½ fl oz water
35g / 1¼ oz butter

Preheat the oven to 200°C / gas mark 6. Line two baking trays with silicon paper. Combine the dry ingredients in a bowl. Melt the butter with the water and bring to the boil. Immediately mix this into the dry ingredients to form a soft dough. Roll out while still warm and cut into squares. Bake one tray at a time for 12 to 15 minutes until they are brown and crisp. Cool on a wire rack.

Variations:
Herb: Add 1 teaspoon fresh chopped rosemary or ½ of dried.
Cranberry: Just use a pinch of salt and add a handful of finely chopped dried cranberries.
Black pepper: Add 1 teaspoon freshly ground black pepper.
Seed: Add 1 tablespoon mixed seeds.

Sesame Sticks

These have a really nutty flavour and go well with creamy cheeses.

1 tbs sesame seeds, toasted
50g / 2oz plain flour
50g / 2oz wholemeal flour
½ tsp salt
2 tsp sesame oil
water to mix
beaten egg

Preheat the oven to 200°C / gas mark 6. Line two baking trays with silicon paper. Combine everything except the egg to make a stiff dough. Roll out quite thin and cut into fingers. Divide between the trays, glaze with egg and bake one tray at a time for 12 to 15 minutes until crisp. Cool on a rack.

Cheese Thins

Including a small proportion of blue cheese is particularly good.

110g / 4oz butter
175g / 6oz plain flour
110g / 4oz mixed cheese, grated
poppy seeds
cracked black pepper

Preheat the oven to 200°C / gas mark 6. Line two baking trays with silicon paper. In a food processor, rub the butter into the flour, add the cheese and process to a smooth dough. Form into a long sausage and roll it in the seeds and pepper. Chill and cut into discs. Bake, one tray at a time, for about 10 minutes until golden. Cool on a rack.

Caraway Biscuits

This recipe makes a lot of dough but I decided not to scale it down as it is difficult to halve an egg accurately and in this recipe accuracy is important. If you don't want to cook it all at once, which would take several batches, the remainder will freeze. We make it in a food processor but it is fine rubbed in with your fingers the old-fashioned way.

150g / 5oz butter
175g / 6oz wholemeal flour
175g / 6oz plain flour
1 tsp sea salt flakes
50g / 2oz demerara sugar
1 tsp caraway seeds plus more for the top
50ml / 2 fl oz water
1 egg, beaten

Preheat the oven to 220°C / gas mark 7. Line two baking trays with silicon paper. Process the butter into the flours until it looks like fine breadcrumbs. Add the salt and sugar and 1 teaspoon of caraway seeds and pulse to just mix (you want to retain the crunchy texture). Beat the egg and water together. Pulse in the liquid to make a firm dough. Roll out to ½ cm / ⅙ in thick. Sprinkle with caraway and press gently with the rolling pin. Cut into small triangles. Bake in batches for about 12 minutes until beginning to brown. Outer biscuits may darken faster so take them off and return the rest for a few minutes. They do need to be crisp or else they won't keep well. Cool on a rack.

Knäckebröd

This seeded Swedish rye crispbread is flaky and crisp. You can use wholemeal flour instead of the rye if you prefer, or a mix of the two. In Sweden they use a brand of sea salt flavoured with herbs which is well worth trying if you can get it. The method sounds like a fiddle but it is really quite straight forward. For the Dining Room we make small wedge shaped biscuits as explained but traditionally they are baked as larger circles and broken apart randomly.

140ml / ¼ pint whole milk or milk and cream mix
70g / 2½ oz rye flour
85g / 3oz strong white flour
¼ tsp salt
½ packet dried yeast (1 heaped teaspoon)
to sprinkle: sea salt, sesame seeds, linseeds, sunflower seeds, poppy seeds, caraway and cumin seeds.

Heat the milk to blood temperature. Mix the flours, salt and yeast and stir in the milk until it is all combined. Leave in a warm place for about 20 minutes. Turn the mixture onto a surface sprinkled with rye flour and knead to a soft dough. Cut into six and roll each piece into a ball. Leave for another 15 minutes. Place a baking tray in the oven and preheat to 240°C / gas mark 9. Cut 6 pieces of silicon paper each about 15cm / 6in square. Roll each ball into a 10cm / 4in circle and transfer to a paper. Sprinkle the circles with the salt and any combination of seeds that you like. Be sparing if using cumin seeds as they are very strong but quite delicious. Roll out again to make the seeds stick so making the dough thinner. Mark into wedges (without cutting right through). When the oven is fully hot, remove the baking tray and slide as many circles as you can fit, off the paper and on to the tray. They should start to bubble slightly. Bake for 5 minutes, turn and bake 3 more. When all are cooked, remove to a rack and turn off the oven. Break up into the marked wedge shapes and after about 5 minutes put the rack onto the floor of the oven. Leave for about 30 minutes to crisp up. They must be stored in an air tight box.

Porridge Oatcakes

When we started to need certified gluten free oats they were much easier to obtain as rolled oats rather than cut oatmeal so we created this recipe. Thin and crispy, they are quite different from our other oatcakes

150g / 5oz rolled oats, ground fine
85g / 3oz rolled oats
1 heaped tsp soft brown sugar
½ tsp salt
25g / 1oz butter, melted
boiling water

Preheat the oven to 190°C / gas mark 5. Line two baking trays with silicon paper. Mix the dry ingredients in a bowl. Pour in the butter and enough boiling water to make a medium dough. Knead lightly and cut into 8. Roll into saucer sized rounds and cut each into quarters. Bake for 20 minutes until crisp. Cool on a rack.

Norwegian Flat Bread

In Norway these are made with 'kulturmelk' which is like a drinking yoghurt.

95g / 3½ oz wholemeal flour
60g / 2¼ oz plain flour
½ flat tsp salt
1 tbs sour cream plus milk to make 125ml / scant ¼ pint in total
plain flour for kneading and rolling
olive oil for frying

Mix the flours, salt, and cream and milk mixture together to make a dough. Knead with a little more flour until smooth and firm. Cover with cling film and leave in a cool place for an hour or more.
Cut into 6, and roll out as thin as you can, they need to be almost see through. If you have a pasta roller this is ideal. We put them through ours working up to the thinnest setting. Leave the rolled pieces to rest on a tray. Brush a pan with olive oil and fry the breads quickly on each side. Remove to a rack. When they are all done, put on a large oven tray and dry out in the oven on the coolest setting available, turning and moving around occasionally. They can take anything from half an hour to two hours. Keep an eye on them. Cool on a rack. Break up and keep in an airtight box.

Water Biscuits

These should be as thin as possible and really crisp.

110g / 4oz self-raising flour
1 tbs olive oil
60ml / 2 fl oz cold water
sea salt flakes

Preheat the oven to 200°C / gas mark 6. Mix the flour, oil and water to make a stiff dough. Allow to rest for a few minutes. Roll on a floured board as thin as possible. Rest a little and roll some more! Sprinkle with salt and roll again to push the salt into the dough. Cut with a small round cutter and lay on baking trays. Bake one tray at a time for 10 to 12 minutes until lightly browned and crisp. Cool on a rack and store in an airtight container.

Rosemary Crackers

100g / 3½ oz plain flour
½ tsp baking powder
good pinch salt
1 dsp fresh chopped rosemary
60ml / 2 fl oz water
olive oil for brushing
sea salt flakes for sprinkling

Preheat the oven to 180°C / gas mark 4. Mix everything together to make a soft dough and knead until smooth. Roll out to a 13cm / 5in square, cut into oblongs and place on a baking tray. Brush with olive oil and sprinkle with salt. Bake for 20 minutes or until starting to brown at the edges. They should still be flaky.

chutneys and relishes

These give that extra something to our cheeseboard and we are always trying different combinations. Simple apple jelly flavoured with fresh garden herbs is another favourite. The chutneys also feature in our packed lunch rolls.

Piccalilli

Home-made piccalilli is a whole different ball game to the bought variety and I highly recommend it.

1 cauliflower
3 onions
3 large carrots
1 cucumber
200g / 7oz French beans
110g / 4oz salt
3 tbs plain flour
2 tsp mild curry powder
2 tsp ground turmeric
1½ tbs mustard powder
4 tsp ground ginger
550g / 1¼ lb sugar
1.14 litres / 2 pints white vinegar

Cut all the vegetables into small dice no bigger than 1cm / ⅓in and place in a non-metallic bowl. Mix in the salt and leave overnight. Rinse the salted vegetables thoroughly with cold water and dry with a clean tea towel. Sift the flour and spices into a large pan and make a smooth paste with a little vinegar. Add the rest of the vinegar and the sugar and bring to the boil, stirring all the time while it thickens. Add the vegetables and boil for a further 2 minutes. Pack into sterile jars.

Sweet and Sour Onion Marmalade

A really unusual condiment that goes beautifully with cheese and charcuterie.

450g / 1lb onions, halved and finely sliced
2 tbs salt
710ml / 1¼ pints white wine vinegar
450g / 1lb sugar
2 tsp cardamom seeds
zest 1 orange

Place the onions in a colander and sprinkle with the salt. Mix well and set aside for 30 minutes. Mix the vinegar and sugar in a large heavy-based pan and bring to the boil. Reduce the heat and allow to bubble gently until it turns golden brown. Remove from the heat. Thoroughly rinse the onions for at least 3 minutes, squeeze dry and stir into the sugar and vinegar. Add the cardamom and zest, bring to the boil and simmer gently for 20 to 30 minutes, stirring often. Remove from the heat, cool slightly, give a final stir, pour into sterile jars and seal.

Apple Chutney

When we have a good apple year in the garden Jane goes into mass chutney production which will see us through the lean years.

1.8kg / 4lb cooking apples, peeled and cored
700g / 1½ lb onions, peeled
1.14 litres / 1½ pints malt vinegar
450g / 1lb prunes, chopped
450g / 1lb dates, chopped
900g / 2lb sugar
25g / 1oz salt
40g / 1½ oz fresh ginger, peeled and grated
1 tbs ground allspice

Chop the apples and onions finely. Simmer these with the prunes, dates and vinegar until everything is soft. Add the rest and boil carefully, stirring often to avoid burning, for about 20 minutes or until thick. Cool slightly and pack in sterile jars.

Rainbow Chilli Pepper Jelly

700g / 1½ lb sweet peppers, mixed colours, deseeded, finely diced.
110g / 4oz hot chillies, finely diced
50g / 2oz fresh root ginger, grated
430ml / ¾ pint cider or white wine vinegar
1kg / 2lb 3oz sugar
1 packet dry pectin
1 level tsp salt
1 tsp citric acid

Place peppers, chillies and ginger in a pan with the vinegar and bring to the boil. Mix the sugar with the pectin, salt and citric acid then add to the pan. Stir to melt and boil for about 10 minutes or until setting point. Allow to cool for about 10 minutes, stir to distribute the peppers and pot in sterile jars.

Blackcurrant and Port Jelly

900g / 2lb blackcurrants
560ml / 1 pint water
sugar
50ml / 2 fl oz port

Wash the fruit and simmer with the water for one hour until very soft. Strain through a jelly bag or muslin overnight. Measure the juice and add sugar at the rate of 450g / 1lb per 560ml / 1 pint of juice. Boil until setting point. Turn off the heat and stir to disperse the foam. Stir in the port. Pour into sterile jars and seal.

Green Tomato Chutney

450g / 1lb green tomatoes, cored and chopped
450g / 1lb onions, peeled and chopped
225g / 8oz sultanas
225g / 8oz brown sugar
2 tsp salt
1 tsp cayenne pepper
1 tsp cardamom seeds
560ml / 1 pint vinegar

Put everything together in a large heavy-based pan and cook until thick and the vegetables are soft. Cool slightly and pack in sterile jars.

SCOTLAND

Breakfasts

Breakfast at Doune includes our own home-made cereals, seasonal fresh fruit compotes, preserves from the Doune kitchen, home-made bread for toast and some fresh baking to finish off.

Porridge is served twice a week or on request. To make Doune style porridge, Soak pinhead oatmeal over-night with plenty of water and a little salt. In the morning, add a small proportion of medium oatmeal and bring to the boil, whisking often. Simmer gently for at least an hour, stirring and adding water as needed to make smooth, soft 'Goldilocks' porridge.

savoury buffet

We make our own potato cakes etc., but of course the crowning glory of any breakfast here are the eggs from our hens, free to range down to the shore, where they pick choice sand hoppers out of the seaweed, they produce the best eggs I have ever tasted.

Scrambled Eggs

We allow one egg per person as part of a full breakfast and add about 25g / 1oz butter, 1 tablespoon of double cream, and an extra egg yolk for every six people. Lightly beat the eggs, yolks, cream, and a generous amount of seasoning just to break up the albumen but not homogenate everything. Melt the butter in a suitable non-stick pan and add the mixture. Cook over moderate heat, stirring often. As the egg starts to coagulate turn the heat down and gently move the mixture around the pan until it is done to your liking. If your pan holds its heat well you can turn it off a minute or so before the end to keep everything going nice and slow. If you love soft and tender egg be sure to get it out of the pan as soon as it is ready or it will keep getting firmer.

Poached Eggs

In our big pan, we can poach 12 eggs at once. We don't add vinegar or salt, and we don't swirl the water. I'm afraid it's all in the eggs, and the better quality and fresher they are the better your poached eggs will be. A shallow pan will make it easier to get the eggs in and out. Choose one about 7.5cm / 3in deep and wide enough so that your eggs will be quite close together. They seem to cook better 'cuddled up' and won't meld into each other. Fill the pan to a depth of 4cm / 1½ in. Have the water boiling hard and just before putting in the eggs turn it right down to simmer. Just crack them straight in one after another. Once all the eggs are in, turn the heat up again. If it comes back to the boil turn it down again but it's quite likely the eggs will be done by then. To test if they are ready, try to take one out and you will soon see if it is too wobbly! A slotted spoon with the biggest holes you can find will help drain the water efficiently before it reaches your plate or toast. Enjoy.

Oven Omelette

For 6 use: 25g / 1oz butter, 6 eggs, 85ml / 3 fl oz cream, 85ml / 3 fl oz milk, ⅓ tsp salt, 4 chopped spring onions. Preheat the oven to 180°C / gas mark 4. Put the butter in a 1.42 litre / 2½ pint ovenproof dish and place in the oven to melt. Beat the eggs, cream, milk and salt together and add the onions. Pour into the dish and bake for 25 minutes or more until just firm.

Corn Fritters

For 8 good size fritters, we use 110g / 4oz self-raising flour to 1 egg, a pinch of salt and enough milk to make a thick batter. Use the method as for our Scotch Pancakes for a light and tender result and add ½ a tin of sweetcorn and ½ tsp dried sage. Fry using a thin layer of fat in the pan.

Hash Browns

A good floury potato is best for these; we use Maris Piper. Allow 1 piece of potato about the size of a roastie per hash brown. Grate the potato finely (a food processor with a fine grating disc is ideal). Lay out a clean tea towel. Take the potato in your hands and squeeze as hard as you can to remove the moisture then spread it out on the tea towel. Sprinkle with salt, gather up the towel and squeeze again. The more moisture you can remove the crisper the result. Get your pan hot and add enough fat so there is a good layer on the surface. Place mounds of potato into the pan and turn the heat down to low/medium. Cook for about 5 minutes until golden on the bottom. Turn over, making sure there is fat on the surface of the pan where you will turn the hash brown on to, adding more fat as needed. Now, and only now, press down with a slice to flatten the mounds and cook the second side until golden and quite crisp, adjusting the heat as necessary. Drain well on kitchen paper before serving.

Potato Cakes and Tattie Scones

Leftover mash is ideal for these. For Potato Cakes, mix in just enough self-raising flour to enable you to pat it into a shape without it crumbling. Add extra seasoning like ground black pepper or some fresh chopped chives if you like. With a little flour on the surface, form a thick sausage and cut it into discs about 2cm / ¾ in thick. Have enough butter to form a thin layer in the pan and fry gently until nicely browned on both sides. For Tattie Scones you need a lot less potato and much more flour. We use plain flour and add enough to make a firm, pastry like, dough. Roll this out to 0.8cm / ⅓ in thick and cut into circles or triangles. Fry in a lightly greased, heavy-based pan until brown on both sides. Serve warm with butter.

breakfast baking

Just a little 'bite' at the end of breakfast, we are often asked for the recipes for our breakfast 'extras'.

Danish Pastries See our croissant recipe on page 158.

Breakfast Fruit Loaves See our bread recipe on page 156.

Lemon Curd and Oatcakes

This is Mary's granny's recipe and Mary used to serve it every day when she started having guests in her house. We can't keep up with that these days but we try to serve this most Dounie of recipes every week as a breakfast extra with our original oatcakes (page 118). We also serve it in Fresh Fruit Pavlova (page 109) and in a version of Muffins (page 130). It really is the best lemon curd recipe ever!

3 eggs + 1 egg yolk
3 lemons, zest and juice
225g / 8oz sugar
25g / 1oz butter

Finely grate the lemon zest into a heatproof bowl. Add the eggs and yolk and beat well to break up the whites (a stick blender is good for this). Juice the lemons and add to the bowl with the sugar and butter. Place the bowl over simmering water and stir frequently until thick. Cool and transfer to a large sterilized jar. Keep refrigerated.

American Pancakes

Lighter than Scotch Pancakes. Little and big kids alike always choose chocolate sprinkles!

makes 24 small or 12 large
3 eggs, separated
110g / 4oz plain flour
1 heaped tsp baking powder
140ml / 5 fl oz milk
pinch salt
butter for frying

Put the flour, baking powder, egg yolks and milk in a bowl and whisk until smooth. In a separate bowl, whisk the egg whites with the salt until they form stiff peaks, and quickly fold into the batter. Heat a heavy-based frying pan to medium hot and add a knob of butter. Fry spoonfuls until starting to firm up. If you want to add flavourings such as crispy bacon, sweetcorn, berries or chocolate chips, sprinkle them on at this stage and press in so they don't burn when turned. Flip over and fry until golden. Serve with chocolate or berry sauce or maple or golden syrup.

Saffron Buns

This recipe from my Cornish born mum takes me back to childhood holidays. The saffron is fragrant and subtle, as are the spices in the variation.

Makes 20 to 30
25g / 1oz butter
315 ml / 11 fl oz milk
2 good pinches saffron
450g / 1lb strong white flour
1 sachet dried yeast
25g / 1oz sugar
50g / 2oz currants

Line two baking sheets with silicon paper. Melt the butter, add the milk and saffron, and heat until it feels warm to the touch. Mix the flour, yeast, sugar, and currants in a bowl, then mix in the warm liquid. Leave in a warm place for about half an hour or until the dough looks soft and has about doubled in size. Turn the dough onto a floured surface and knead until smooth. Form into long buns and divide between the trays, placing the buns quite close so that as they rise they touch each other. Leave in a warm place until they have doubled again. Heat the oven to 220°C / gas mark 7 and cook for 4 minutes. Swap the trays and cook 4 minutes more. They should be golden brown on the tops with a little colour on the bottoms but still feel soft. Cool on a rack. Best eaten warm with butter.

Variation: Sugar Buns

Omit the saffron and currants. Add 1 tsp ground cinnamon, 1 tbs chopped stem ginger, and 1 dsp of the syrup from the stem ginger jar. Dip the formed buns quickly first in water and then sugar. Place sugar side up.

Scotch Pancakes

I favour the following method for making really light, tender pancakes but it is more traditional to make them smoother by beating hard. Obviously, maple syrup is not an original ingredient but it does impart the right, slightly caramelized, flavour.

makes 8
110g / 4oz self-raising flour
½ tsp baking powder
1 dsp sugar
1 egg
1 dsp maple syrup
milk to mix to a thick batter
butter for greasing

Mix the flour, baking powder, and sugar in a bowl. Whisk the egg and syrup with a little milk. Fold everything together gently adding more milk as required to make a thick batter. There should be no obvious flour but the mixture will look lumpy. Grease a heavy-based pan with a little butter and get it hot. Add dessertspoonfuls of batter and turn the heat down to medium. When bubbles appear, turn over and cook for about 30 seconds more. Cool on a rack for a minute before serving. When cooking the next batch, make sure the pan is hot again to start.

Muffins

Making individual muffins is a fiddly business in the morning and one year Pippa suggested we just make the mixture into a cake – a real breakthrough! Cooling in the tin(s) helps keep them moist.

makes 10 to 12 deep muffins / 1 loaf / 36 mini muffins / 18 shallow buns

250g / 9oz self-raising flour
1 tsp baking powder
¼ tsp salt
85g / 3oz sugar
1 egg
225ml / 8 fl oz milk
85g / 3oz butter, melted

Preheat the oven to 195°C / gas mark 5 to 6. Prepare muffin tins with liners or a standard 900g / 2lb loaf tin by lining with silicon paper. Mix the dry ingredients together with a fork. Beat the egg and liquid ingredients together. Pour the liquid into the dry and mix gently but quickly, no more than 20 seconds. There should be no obvious flour but the batter will be lumpy and this is fine. Pour into your tin(s) and bake for about 20 minutes for the muffins or 30 for a cake until risen and firm to the touch. Leave to cool a little in the tin(s), (the cake is best left for 30 minutes), before serving warm.

Variations:

Many Flavoured Muffins

Poppy seed: (Known at Doune as midge muffins). Add 1 tsp vanilla extract and 1 tbs poppy seeds.

Fresh fruit: Add 1 handful of fresh or frozen berries.

Lemon: Add the zest of one lemon and top with teaspoonfuls of lemon curd (page 128).

Chocolate: Add 1 tsp vanilla extract and 1 handful of chocolate chips.

Cranberry and Orange: Add the zest of an orange and 1 handful of dried cranberries.

Scones

Everyone who cooks in the kitchen has their own recipe for scones and we keep changing allegiance. However, for the lightest we have ever tried I would vote for this from the Ballymaloe Cookery School, after all, who would dare tell the Irish how to make scones?!

makes 12

300g / 10½ oz plain flour
pinch salt
1 heaped tsp baking powder
20g / ¾ oz caster sugar
50g / 2oz butter
1 egg, beaten
140ml / 5 fl oz milk
caster sugar for the tops

Preheat the oven to 230°C / gas mark 8 and sprinkle a metal baking sheet with flour. Rub the dry ingredients with the butter until it resembles breadcrumbs. Whisk together the egg and milk. Reserve 1 tablespoon of this and stir the rest into the flour mix. Pull the dough together with your hands and pat out to 2.5cm / 1in thick. Cut with a sharp knife or round cutter. Use the spare egg mix to brush the tops then sprinkle liberally with the caster sugar. Place on the baking sheet and bake for 10 to 12 minutes until golden brown on top.

Welsh Cakes

A recipe from Andy's mum who was a great baker. Being a richer mix than English griddle scones they are more prone to burning, so using a griddle or very heavy-based pan and turning as low as possible is very important. They are super delicious!

makes 12 to 16
225g / 8oz self-raising flour
½ tsp salt
110g / 4oz butter
50g / 2oz sugar
50g / 2oz currants
1 egg, beaten
2 tbs milk
butter for greasing

Rub the butter into the flour and salt. Add the rest and mix to a stiff dough. On a floured surface, pat the dough down to 1.25cm / ½ in thick and cut into segments, or use a round cutter. Grease a heavy based pan with a little butter and get it hot. Turn the heat as low as it will go and place the Welsh Cakes on the pan. Cook until turning brown on the underside and starting to go firm. Turn and continue cooking without increasing the heat until they are firm to the touch. Cool on a rack for a minute or two and serve warm with butter.

Crumpets

One giant crumpet is so much easier than fiddling about with individual rings. Our pan is 30.5cm / 12in. Two smaller pans would do fine. It is not necessary to do the greaseproof paper trick, but it is fun! The wedges freeze well.

makes 16 wedges
150g / 5oz strong white flour
150g / 5oz plain flour
1½ sachets dried yeast
¾ tsp salt
¾ tsp sugar
255ml / 9 fl oz milk
155ml / 5½ fl oz water
½ tsp bicarbonate of soda
¾ tsp white wine vinegar
butter for frying

Whisk together the flours, yeast, salt and sugar. Gently heat the milk and water so it is warm to the touch and add to the flour. Whisk until smooth. Leave in a warm place until it doubles in size and is bubbling nicely. Mix the bicarb and vinegar and whisk into the batter. Set a non-stick pan (as above) on a low heat and add a knob of butter. Swirl the melted butter around and pour in the batter. Cook on low for 15 to 20 minutes until bubbles are showing well and it is almost firm except for a thin layer on the top. Lay some greaseproof or baking paper over the top then pull it off to reveal the bubble holes. Continue cooking until it is completely set. Slide the cooked crumpet out onto a rack to cool. Cut into wedges and toast on both sides to serve.

breakfast cereals

These are our combinations but feel free to substitute any nut or fruit you like or change the balance of grains to nuts etc. I would definitely recommend tracking down Lexia raisins which have a fabulous fresh, fruity flavour.

Plain Muesli

225g / 8oz porridge oats
225g / 8oz wheat flakes
2 tbs each of hazels, brazils, cashews, flaked almonds
12 each of dates, orange apricots, dark apricots, all rough chopped
2 tbs each of Lexia raisins, Chilean Flame raisins, sultanas
1 tbs each of pumpkin seeds, sunflower seeds

Mix everything together and store in an airtight container.

Granola

2½ tbs peanut oil or melted coconut oil
1 large pinch salt
3½ tbs maple or golden syrup
3½ tbs runny honey
¼ tsp cinnamon
1 egg white
125g / 4½ oz porridge oats
125g / 4½ oz wheat flakes
50g / 2oz broken walnuts
50g / 2oz hazelnuts
25g / 1oz flaked almonds
25g / 1oz sunflower seeds
25g / 1oz sesame seeds

Line a large roasting tin or baking tray with a lip with silicon paper. Preheat the oven to 170°C / gas mark 3. In a large bowl, whisk the oil, salt, syrup, honey, cinnamon and egg white well together and stir in the rest. Spread on the tray to make an even layer and bake for approximately 45 minutes until crisp. After about 30 minutes, without breaking up the mixture too much, move the outer bits that are starting to brown into the centre and and push the paler bits to the outside. Return to the oven. This ensures that nothing gets burnt and the granola is an even toasty brown colour. Cool on the tray and then break up into nuggets. Store in an airtight container.

Toasted Muesli

225g / 8oz porridge oats
225g / 8oz wheat flakes
4 tbs raw peanuts
2 tbs each of hazels, cashews, pumpkin seeds, sunflower seeds
2 tbs peanut or melted coconut oil
2 tbs runny honey
2 tbs Lexia raisins
2 tbs orange apricots, rough chopped

In a roasting tin, mix together everything except the fruit. Bake until rich brown and toasted, stirring occasionally. Any temperature is fine but long and slow is easier. We often have it at the bottom of the oven while something else is baking above. Cool, add the prepared fruit and store in an airtight container.

breakfast preserves

We always serve our traditional marmalade plus two other different preserves every day. Over a seven day period that is a lot of varieties and given our policy of ringing the changes each year, we now have a big selection of recipes to choose from! Here are some of our favourites.

Steve's Honey Marmalade

A recipe from Steve who comes every year to help us get ready for the season, and if we are very lucky, he brings some of his beautiful honey with him!

makes 8 or 9 jars
1.35kg / 3lb Seville oranges
1 apple
1.14 litres / 2 pints water
juice 2 lemons
1.35kg / 3lb sugar
1 sachet dry pectin
1.35kg / 3lb runny honey

Juice the oranges, scoop out the pith and cut up the skins, Put the pith and seeds in a muslin bag. Peel, core and blend the apple. Put the bag, peel, apple and water in the pressure cooker and cook at high pressure for 8 minutes. Reduce pressure slowly. Dry mix the sugar and pectin in a preserving pan. Add the peel and remaining liquid from the pressure cooker. Push the contents of the bag through a sieve; you will be left with the pips and tougher bits of pulp which you can dispose of. Add the sieved pulp and lemon juice to the preserving pan. Bring gently to the boil and boil hard for 4 minutes. It should come to jam temperature. Take off the heat and stir to disperse the foam. Cool a little and add the honey, stirring well. Pot into warm sterile jars.

Bramble and Blackcurrant Jam

makes 8 to 9 jars
1.8kg / 4lb brambles
430ml / ¾ pint water
1 tsp citric acid
900g / 2lb blackcurrants
850ml / 1½ pints water
1.35kg / 3lb sugar
extra sugar per juice

Simmer the brambles, citric acid and the first lot of water for about I hour until really soft. Strain through a jelly bag overnight and measure the juice. Simmer the blackcurrants gently with the second lot of water until soft and reduced by half. Add the bramble juice. Add the sugar plus 450g per 560ml of juice. (1lb per pint.) Boil hard to setting point (about 15 minutes). Turn off the heat and stir to disperse the foam. Pot into warm sterile jars.

Rhubarb and Vanilla Preserve

We make this in small amounts as it doesn't keep well. It is a soft set.

makes 2 jars
250g / 9oz rhubarb
150g / 5oz sugar
1 vanilla bean, split lengthwise
2 tbs water

Heat all together gently until the sugar is melted. Simmer until thick (10 to 20 minutes). Remove the bean and pot in sterilised jars.

Spiced Apple Jelly

makes 5 to 6 jars
1.8kg / 4lb hard sour apples
1 tsp whole cloves
water to cover
2 tbs black or redcurrants
1 tsp citric acid
sugar

Wash and roughly chop the fruit, (no need to peel or core), and simmer with the water for one hour until very soft. Strain through a jelly bag or muslin overnight. Measure the juice and add the citric acid; it should make about 1.28 litres / 2¼ pints and if it is over then reduce it to this amount. Add sugar at the rate of 450g per 560ml of liquid. (1lb per pint.) Boil until setting point is reached. Turn off the heat and stir to disperse the foam. Pot into warm sterile jars.

Gooseberry and Elderflower Jam

makes 4 to 5 jars
900g / 2lb gooseberries
140ml / 5 fl oz water
900g / 2lb sugar
4 tbs elderflower cordial

Simmer the gooseberries and water gently for 15 minutes. Over about 15 minutes on a very low heat, dissolve the sugar in the fruit. Bring to a hard boil and boil for 8 minutes. Test for set and boil a little more if needed. Cool slightly and stir in the cordial. Pot in warm sterile jars.

Whisky Marmalade

Adding the whisky just as you turn off the heat means that the harsh alcohol is driven off but the flavour is retained. You can use any whisky but we think one with strongly peaty notes works well. Happily, our 'local' malt, Talisker Skye, fits the bill.

makes 8-9 jars
1.35kg / 3lb Seville oranges
juice 2 lemons
850ml / 1½ pints water
2.7kg / 6lb sugar
1 sachet dry pectin
6 tbs whisky

Juice the oranges and scrape out the white pith. Cut the peel into long thin shreds. Put the pith and seeds in a muslin bag and tie with string. Either put the bag, peel, lemon juice and 850ml / 1½ pints of water in a pressure cooker and cook at high pressure for 10 minutes. Or put the bag, peel, lemon juice and 3.36 litres / 6 pints of water in a very large pan and simmer until the volume is reduced by half. Mix the sugar and pectin together. In a bowl, weigh the cooked peel and liquid. Squeeze as much moisture as you can from the bag and add this to the bowl. Make up to 2.475kg / 5½ lb with extra water if needed. (Or boil more to reduce to this weight.) Put into a preserving pan with the sugar and pectin and bring to the boil. Boil hard until jam temperature is reached or until it is wrinkling well on a cold plate. This takes about half an hour. Take off the heat and stir to disperse the foam. Immediately add the whisky and stir. Cool a little before jarring in warm sterile jars.

Peach Melba Jam

It really does take very few raspberries to give the subtle raspberry note to this stunning peach jam.

makes 4-5 jars
1.175kg / 2lb 10oz fresh ripe peaches
280ml / ½ pint water
2 lemons, rind and juice
175g / 6oz raspberries
900g / 2lb sugar
¾ packet dried pectin

To peel the peaches, have ready a large bowl of iced water. Place the whole peaches in a pan full of boiling water and leave for 45 seconds. Remove and put immediately into the iced water. Peel, stone and slice the peaches and put in a large pan with the measured water. Pare the yellow zest from the lemons in large pieces and add to the pan. Simmer until the fruit is soft and the water well reduced. Remove the zest and add the lemon juice and raspberries. Mix the pectin with the sugar and add to the pan. Heat gently until the sugar has dissolved and then boil hard for about 5 minutes or until setting point is reached. Turn off the heat and stir to disperse the foam. Pot into warm sterile jars.

Raspberry and Redcurrant Jam

makes 8 to 9 jars
1.35kg / 3lb redcurrants
560ml / 1 pint water
1.35kg / 3lb raspberries
1.35kg / 3lb sugar
extra sugar for extract

Simmer the redcurrants with the water until the fruit as very soft. Strain through a jelly bag overnight and measure the juice. Simmer the raspberries gently for a few minutes until they give up plenty of juice but try to keep some fruit whole. Add the redcurrant juice. Add the sugar plus 450g per 560ml of juice. (1lb per pint.) Boil hard to setting point (about 15 minutes). Turn off the heat and stir to disperse the foam. Pot into warm sterile jars.

Ginger and Lemon Preserve

A great way to use up that courgette that got missed and turned into a marrow overnight!

makes 6 jars
1.35kg / 3lb prepared marrow
85g / 3oz fresh ginger
2 lemons, fine zest and juice
1.35kg / 3lb sugar
3 tbs stem ginger, finely chopped
zest 1 lemon

Cut the marrow into 1.25cm / ½ in cubes, boil until it is soft and drain well. Thinly slice the ginger and tie it in a muslin bag. In a large pan, boil the marrow, ginger, zest, juice, and sugar for 30 minutes. Remove the ginger bag and mash or blend the marrow - it doesn't need to be totally smooth. Add the stem ginger and extra lemon zest. Cool slightly and jar in warm sterile jars.

Sloe Gin Jelly

Sloes don't grow well in this area, the soil is too acid. However, if I travel away at the end of the season, I am always on the lookout, and often come back with a bag full for sloe gin making. It seems such a waste to throw away the sloes once the liqueur is drained off, and a chance discussion with a guest led me to find a way to use them.

makes 6 jars
1.8kg / 4lb hard sour apples
700g / 1½ lb sloes from sloe gin making
juice I lemon
1 good glug sloe gin
sugar

Wash and roughly chop the apples, put in a pan with the sloes, cover well with water and simmer for one hour until very soft. Strain through a jelly bag or muslin overnight and add the lemon juice and sloe gin. Measure the juice; it should make about 1.57 litres / 2¾ pints and if it is over then reduce it to this. Add sugar at the rate of 450g per 560ml of juice. (1lb per pint.) Boil until setting point is reached. Turn off the heat and stir to disperse the foam. Pot into warm sterile jars.

Baking

Our baking recipes are mostly for guest packed lunches so need to be reasonably sturdy and 'packable'. Tray bakes are really good for packing and we have found that many of the cakes also work well cooked in trays, making them faster to bake, easier to cut and a better shape for wrapping.

Note:
Recipes are worked out using **large eggs**. We always choose free range. All **spoon measures** are rounded unless otherwise stated.

tray bakes

Mochaccino Slice

A really unusual recipe with a rich toffee flavour. The original idea came from a magazine years ago but we have made so many changes we feel it is our own.

makes 18
for the base:
110g / 4oz butter
225g / 8oz digestive biscuits, crushed finely
110g / 4oz white chocolate chips
for the top:
110g / 4oz butter
225g / 8oz dark brown sugar
2 eggs plus 1 egg yolk, beaten
2 tsp instant coffee powder
150g / 5oz self-raising flour
1 tsp baking powder
60g / 2½ oz white chocolate chips

Preheat the oven to 180°C / gas mark 4. Line a 30x23cm / 12x9in traybake tin with silicon paper.
For the base, melt the butter and mix in the biscuits. Press into the tin and sprinkle on the white chocolate chips. For the topping, melt the butter and mix in the sugar. Beat in the eggs and fold in the coffee powder, flour and baking powder. Pour onto the biscuit base and sprinkle the chocolate chips evenly over the top. Bake for 40 minutes and cool in the tin.

Jamie's Flapjack

Mary tells the story of Jamie as a toddler sitting on the kitchen table helping her with the baking and together they invented this no syrup flapjack. I can't help thinking her memory is a little clouded by nostalgia, certainly, my toddler never sat still long enough to achieve this kind of thing but maybe Mary and Jamie are made of sterner stuff. However, we have the flapjack recipe and it wouldn't be summer at Doune without the smell of it wafting from the kitchen.

makes 18
225g / 8oz butter
225g / 8oz soft brown sugar
450g / 1lb rolled porridge oats

Preheat the oven to 180°C / gas mark 4. Line a 30x23cm / 12x9in traybake tin with silicon paper.
In a large pan, gently melt the butter and sugar. Add the oats and mix well. Spread in the tin, pressing gently with a clean metal spoon. Bake for 15 to 20 minutes until bubbling at the edges but when you tilt the tin it is still flowing in the centre. Cut while it is still warm but leave to cool in the tin.

Gisela's Apple Crumble Cake

This recipe came from a wonderful friend and many times visitor to Doune. It is quite moist so doesn't keep well but that won't be a problem as it is fiendishly delicious. You can add a few fresh brambles in season but don't overpower the apple which is the real star of the show. Use extra apple and it is brilliant as a family pudding with custard.

makes 18 pieces

for the dough:

250g / 9oz plain cake flour
½ sachet dried yeast
50g / 2oz sugar
Pinch salt
50g / 2oz butter, melted
125ml / 4½ fl oz milk
1 egg

for the topping:

2 very large cooking apples or equivalent
250g / 9oz plain flour
110g / 4oz sugar
½ tsp salt
185g / 6½ oz butter

Line a 30x23cm / 12x9in traybake tin with silicon paper. To make the base, mix the flour, yeast, sugar and salt in a large bowl. Beat together the melted butter, milk and egg. Pour the liquid into the dry mixture, beat well with a wooden spoon and spread into the prepared tin. Peel and core the apples, cut each into 16 slices and lay over the base. Make a crumble with the rest by rubbing it all together with your fingers and spread it over the apple. Leave to rise in a warm place for 2½ hours. Preheat the oven to 200°C / gas mark 6. Bake for 35 minutes. Allow to cool just a little before turning out onto a board. Peel off the paper and turn back quickly onto a rack to finish cooling.

Coconut Slice

Inspired by a Sue Lawrence recipe, pretty much every year the staff vote this as the best baking recipe we do; what more need I say?

makes 18 pieces

350g / 12oz digestive biscuits, crushed but not completely fine
150g / 5oz butter
225g / 8oz chocolate, chopped
175g / 6oz desiccated coconut
1 tin (397g) condensed milk

Preheat the oven to 180°C / gas mark 4. Line a 30x23cm / 12x9in traybake tin with silicon paper.
In a large pan, melt the butter and condensed milk together gently. Cool a little. Mix in the digestives, chocolate and 110g / 4oz of the coconut. Press well into the tin. Sprinkle the rest of the coconut on top, pressing down lightly. Bake for 20 minutes. The coconut topping should be lightly coloured. Cool in the tin before cutting.

Variation:

Lemon Coconut Slice

Add the zest of a lemon and use white chocolate instead of dark.

Peanut Bars

New for the 2017 season this started as biscuits and ended up as a very yummy tray bake.

makes 18
125g / 4½ oz soft butter
150g / 5oz peanut butter
225g / 8oz granulated sugar
1 egg, beaten
150g / 5oz self-raising flour
110g / 4oz raw whole peanuts, roughly chopped
a little demerara sugar

Preheat the oven to 180°C / gas mark 4. Line a 30x23cm / 12x9in traybake tin with silicon paper. Cream the butter and peanut butter together. Beat in the sugar. Mix in the egg, flour, and most of the peanuts. Pour into the tin and spread to the edges. Sprinkle with demerara sugar and the rest of the chopped nuts, and press in lightly. Bake for 25 minutes then reduce the oven temperature to 150 °C / gas mark 2 and bake a further 10 minutes. Cool in the tin

Chocolate Orange Flapjack

An unusual flapjack and really good for packing.

makes 18 pieces
175g / 6oz butter
110g / 4oz dark chocolate chips
3 tbs golden syrup
175g / 6oz granulated sugar
1 tbs cocoa
zest 1 orange
450g / 1lb porridge oats

Preheat the oven to 180°C / gas mark 4. Line a 30x23cm / 12x9in traybake tin with silicon paper.
In a large pan, melt the butter, chocolate, syrup and sugar gently together. Add the rest of the ingredients and mix well. Turn into the tin and spread out with the back of a clean metal spoon. Bake for 20 to 25 minutes. It should be bubbling but still flowing. Allow to cool a little and then cut the pieces but leave in the tin until fully cold.

Variation:

Salted Chocolate Flapjack

Omit the orange, sprinkle with flaked sea salt and press lightly.

Variation:

Chocolate Peanut Flapjack

Omit the orange and add chopped salted roasted peanuts to the mix.

Chocolate Biscuit Slice

There are lots of versions of this no-bake biscuit slice around, but this one from my childhood is hard to beat. The sharpness of the currants and a good dark chocolate mean it is not over sweet but it is still pretty rich so a small piece is enough.

makes 18 to 24
400g / 14oz rich tea or digestive biscuits
225g / 8oz butter
2 tbs soft brown sugar
2 tbs cocoa powder
1½ tbs golden syrup
175g / 6oz currants
400g / 14oz chocolate

Line a 30x23cm / 12x9in traybake tin with silicon paper. Crush the biscuits roughly. Melt the butter, sugar, drinking chocolate, and syrup together in a large pan. Add the currants and biscuits and mix well. Press firmly into the tin. Melt the chocolate gently and spread over the top. Leave in a cool place to set before cutting. Avoid chilling in the fridge as this makes it very hard to cut and can also make the chocolate go cloudy.

Date and Oat Slice

This lovely recipe came from Kathryn who cooked with us in the 2010 season. The apricot version came about when we ran out of dates and has proved to be delicious.

makes 18
350g / 12oz stoned dates
juice 1 lemon
150 ml / ¼ pint water
250g / 9oz butter
250g / 9oz demerara sugar
250g / 9oz rolled oats
250g / 9oz self-raising flour

Preheat the oven to 190°C / gas mark 5. Line a 30x23cm / 12x9in traybake tin with silicon paper. Mix together the dates, lemon juice and water in a pan and cook for about 5 minutes until soft. It should be a spreadable consistency, you can add a little more water if needed but avoid it being too wet. In a large pan melt the butter and add the sugar, rolled oats and flour, mix well but try to keep it crumbly. Put about half the oat mixture in the tin and press down well. Spread the dates over this base and crumble the remaining oat mixture on top. Bake for about 30 minutes then cover lightly with foil and cook a further 20 minutes until crisp. Cool in the tin.

Variation:

Apricot and Oat Slice

Substitute dried apricots for the dates. In this case use more water, enough to cover the fruit, and simmer for 15 minutes with a tight lid. Cool and blend to make a purée.

Berry and Coconut Traybake

I found this unusual tray bake in a magazine a few years ago. It was, deservedly, a competition winner and we love it for making great use of our homegrown berries. For a special tea or even pudding, make it in a round tin and top with whipped cream and more fresh berries.

makes 18 pieces

250g / 9oz self-raising flour
225g / 8oz butter
25g / 1oz rolled oats
275g / 10oz light soft brown sugar
175g / 6oz desiccated coconut
1 egg, beaten
225g / 8oz any frozen berries, slightly crushed

Preheat the oven to 180°C / gas mark 4. Line a 30x23cm / 12x9in traybake tin with silicon paper. Rub the butter into the flour until it resembles fine breadcrumbs. Turn into a large bowl and stir in the oats, sugar and coconut, Reserve a cupful of this mixture (about 175g / 6oz) and keep aside. Stir the egg into the main mixture and spread over the prepared tin. Smooth over the surface using the back of a damp spoon but don't press too hard. Scatter over the berries and sprinkle the reserved mixture over the top. Bake for about 40 minutes until an inserted skewer comes out with moist crumbs but no wet mixture. Reduce the heat to 180°C / Gas mark 3, cover the cake loosely with foil and continue cooking for 15 to 20 more minutes. Leave to cool in the tin before cutting.

Chocolate and Peanut Munchy

One of our first packed lunch tray bakes and still a huge favourite. The trick is not to overcook; it should still be soft coming out of the oven. If you catch it right it will be moist and munchy. Longer cooking makes it a bit crumbly.

makes 18

175g / 6oz butter
2 tbs golden syrup
110g / 4oz granulated sugar
85g / 3oz sultanas
85g / 3oz raw peanuts
110g / 4oz rolled oats
175g / 6oz self-raising flour
110g / 4oz chocolate drops

Preheat the oven to 180°C / gas mark 4. Line a 30x23cm / 12x9in traybake tin with silicon paper.
In a large pan, melt the butter, syrup and sugar gently. Take off the heat and add the sultanas, peanuts, oats and flour. Mix well, then add the chocolate drops and mix again briefly. Spread into the prepared tray and bake for 20 to 25 minutes. Leave to cool in the tray then cut into pieces.

Variation: Walnut Munchy

Substitute the golden syrup with 1 tbs honey and 1 tbs black treacle. Use walnuts instead of peanuts and use white chocolate instead of dark.

biscuits

Grantham Gingerbreads

This is one of Mary's granny's recipes and Mary has fond memories of eating them as a child, but only on special occasions. The ingredients are in unusual proportions but stick with it as they work really well. The key is in the cooking, they should not be completely crisp, rather slightly gooey in the middle, Mary is very specific about this. (And I'm not sure she wholly approves of my variations!)

makes 16 large biscuits
70g / 2¾ oz well softened butter
225g / 8oz granulated sugar
zest ½ lemon
1 egg
225g / 8oz self-raising flour
1 tsp ground ginger

Preheat the oven to 170°C / gas mark 3. Line two baking trays with silicon paper. Cream the butter, sugar and lemon zest until really soft. Add the egg and beat well. Work in the flour and ginger; the mixture will be very stiff. Turn on to a floured work surface and form into a sausage. Cut into 16 pieces and place, well spaced out, on the two baking sheets, (you don't need to press them flat, they will spread themselves). Use the middle shelf and the one two racks below or equivalent in your oven. Bake for 8 minutes and then swap the trays and bake 8 minutes more. Take out when risen and cracking and just faintly coloured; they should be slightly soft in the middle. Leave for a few minutes before removing from the tray and cool on wire racks.

Variation: Almond Cookies

Omit the lemon and ground ginger and add a few drops of almond extract, 50g / 2oz flaked almonds and 50g / 2oz whole almonds.

Variation: Chocolate Chip Cookies

Omit the lemon and ground ginger and add a few drops of vanilla extract and 110g / 4oz dark chocolate chips.

Dark Chocolate Cookies

These rich, crunchy biscuits come from New Zealand. They are seriously chocolatey and although rather too crumbly for packing they are way too good to be left out. They make a great teatime biscuit. A few white chocolate squiggles as well as the dark looks really stunning.

makes 20 small
150g / 5oz plain flour
2 level tbs cocoa
175g / 6oz well softened butter
110g / 4oz caster sugar
½ tsp vanilla essence
50g / 2oz slightly crushed cornflakes
85g / 3oz dark chocolate for topping

Preheat the oven to 180°C / gas mark 4. Line two baking trays with silicon paper. Sift the flour and cocoa together. Cream the butter, sugar and vanilla until really soft. Work in the flour and cocoa and mix in the cornflakes. Place in 20 heaps on the baking trays and press down slightly. Bake for 10 minutes and then swap the trays and bake 10 minutes more. They should be crisp. Leave a few minutes before lifting off the baking trays then cool on a wire rack. Top with squiggles of melted chocolate

Coconut Oaties

We have been making these delicious biscuits for about 20 years but it took us half that time to realize that they are a well known Australian recipe called Anzac Cookies. We make them extra large for packed lunches.

makes 30 small
110g / 4oz plain flour
175g / 6oz granulated sugar
85g / 3oz coconut
85g / 3oz rolled oats
95g / 3½ oz butter
40g / 1½ oz golden syrup (1 tbs)
½ tsp bicarbonate of soda
50g / 2oz boiling water (2 tbs)

Line two baking trays with silicon paper. Preheat the oven to 175°C / between gas marks 3 and 4.
Mix the flour sugar, coconut and oats. Melt the butter and syrup. Add the bicarbonate of soda to the boiling water. Mix everything together and put well-spaced spoonfuls (the mixture may spread) on the trays. (If your trays are small, you may want to cook in two batches.) Press down very slightly. Bake both trays at once, one on the middle shelf and the other two shelves below or equivalent in your oven. Bake for 9 minutes then swap the trays and cook 7 to 9 minutes more. They should be starting to brown. Cool slightly before lifting on to a rack to complete cooling.

Cornish Fairings

These are a memory from my childhood and when we came across the recipe we had to try it. The biscuits are melt in the mouth crispy with a distinctive cracked surface. It took us a while to perfect the baking process and get them just right. It's a bit of a performance but worth it. It is also crucial to weigh as accurately as possible.

makes 16 small

110g / 4oz plain flour
pinch salt
1 level tsp baking powder
1 level tsp bicarbonate of soda
1 level tsp ground ginger
½ level tsp mixed spice
50g / 2oz butter
50g / 2oz sugar
50g / 2oz golden syrup

Preheat the oven to 200°C / gas mark 6. Line two baking trays with silicon paper. Sift the dry ingredients together. Rub in the butter and add the sugar. Warm the syrup slightly, add to the rest and mix well to make a fairly stiff paste. Roll into a sausage and cut into 16. Place, well spaced out as the mixture will spread, on the two lined baking trays. Use the middle shelf and the one two racks below or equivalent in your oven. Bake for 5 minutes and then swap the trays and bake 4 more minutes. Turn the oven off and leave for 5 minutes. Swap the trays again and leave for a further 5 minutes. Remove and cool on a rack. They do need to be kept in an airtight container.

Variation: Nutty Fairings

Omit the ginger and spice and add 50g / 2oz mixed chopped nuts.

Variation: Chocolate Fairings

Omit the ginger and spice. Use just 60g / 2½ oz flour and 40g / 1½ oz cocoa powder.

cakes

Cherry and Pistachio Cake

This is based on a recipe from the Ballymaloe Cookery School. The ingredient mahleb is ground cherry stones and hails from the Middle East. I'm sure you could make it without but it does lend an unusual delicate, aromatic, slightly bitter almond flavour. It is fantastic with fresh plums and fresh cherries but since these are only available for a short season we tried dried sour cherries and they work really well. (Don't use normal glacé cherries as these are too sweet.) Using a 23cm / 9in round tin looks lovely for a tea time cake, it will take a little longer to cook as it will be slightly thicker. To make a superb gluten free cake, substitute the flour for ground almonds and the ground almonds for cornflour. Add 1 tsp gluten free baking powder.

makes 18 pieces
125g / 4½ oz sugar
110g / 4oz light brown sugar
225g / 8oz self-raising flour, sifted
40g / 1¼ oz ground pistachios
70g / 2½ oz desiccated coconut
70g / 2½ oz ground almonds
good pinch salt
1½ tsp ground mahleb
185g / 6½ oz butter, melted
4 eggs, beaten
175g / 6oz dried sour cherries or 350g / 12oz fresh cherries or plums (stones removed, plums halved)
50g / 2oz rough chopped pistachios for the top

Preheat the oven to 180°C / gas mark 4. Line a 30x23cm / 12x9in traybake tin with silicon paper. Mix the first eight ingredients together in a large bowl. Add the melted butter and eggs and mix well. Spoon the mixture into the lined tin and smooth down. Drop the dried cherries (or fresh cherries or plums) onto the mixture and sprinkle the top of the cake with the roughly chopped pistachios. Bake for 45 to 55 minutes or until an inserted skewer comes out clean. Cool in the tin.

Simnel Cake

To make it easier to cut for packed lunches, we make this traditional simnel cake recipe as a long loaf with the marzipan, (made into a slightly flattened sausage), running through the middle. The round version here is how my mum made it when I was a child, with an extra layer of uncooked marzipan on the top and Easter decorations.

makes 1 round cake
175g / 6oz soft butter
175g / 6oz sugar
3 eggs, beaten
225g / 8oz self-raising flour
2 tsp mixed spice
a little milk
350g / 12oz currants
110g / 4oz sultanas
85g / 3oz mixed peel
250g / 9oz marzipan plus the same again if you want to decorate.

Preheat the oven to 170°C / gas mark 3. Line a 20cm / 8in deep cake tin with silicon or greaseproof paper. Cream the butter and sugar well and mix in the eggs, flour and spice. Add a little milk to a make soft consistency and mix in the dried fruit. Put half of the mixture into the lined tin. Flatten the marzipan into a circle to fit the tin and lay it on the mixture. Add the rest of the mixture and spread it flat. Bake for 1 hour. Turn down the oven to 150 °C / gas mark 2 and bake a further ¾ to 1 hour. It should be firm to the touch. (The standard skewer test is tricky as the marzipan in the middle will be gooey.) Cool in the tin.

Honey and Ginger Cake

This is a lovely sticky cake and is based on one of Mary's inventions. Something a bit different to the standard dark ginger cake.

makes 18
110g / 4oz butter
50g / 2oz golden syrup
85g / 3oz honey
110g / 4oz granulated sugar
285g / 10½ oz plain flour
110g / 4oz sultanas
1 tsp bicarbonate of soda
¾ tsp ground ginger
1 egg, beaten
240ml / 8 fl oz milk
½ tsp vinegar
1 tbs stem ginger shavings with syrup

Preheat the oven to 170°C / gas mark 3. Line a 30x23cm / 12x9in traybake tin with silicon paper. Weigh the syrup, honey, butter and sugar into a pan and melt gently. Sift the flour, bicarbonate of soda, and ginger into a large bowl and stir in the sultanas. Beat the egg, milk and vinegar together. Add the melted mixture to the dry ingredients and mix until smooth. Gently stir in the milk mixture and ginger shavings until it is all incorporated. Pour into the tray and bake for 35 to 40 minutes or until the cake bounces back when gently pressed. Cool in the tray for a few minutes then turn out.

Armenian Nutmeg Cake

This is a really unusual cake which came to us via Holly, who was with us for the 2013 season. The nutmeg flavour is strong but not overpowering and it is very moreish indeed. Be really generous when sprinkling the granulated sugar as this makes a lovely crispy top. The Jaffa variation is a recent addition and has proved hugely popular!

makes 18 pieces

225g / 8oz self-raising flour
225g / 8oz plain flour
1 tsp ground nutmeg
110g / 4oz butter
350g / 12oz light soft brown sugar
110g / 4oz chopped walnuts
1 tsp bicarbonate of soda
1 egg, beaten
milk to make a soft consistency, about 280ml / ½ pint
granulated sugar for sprinkling

Preheat the oven to 190°C / gas mark 5. Line a 30x23cm / 12x9in traybake tin with silicon paper.
Put the flours, nutmeg, butter and brown sugar in a large bowl and rub gently between your fingers until it resembles breadcrumbs. Put 350g / 12oz of this mixture into the tin and press it firmly with the back of a spoon. Whisk the egg and bicarb. with the milk and add to the remaining dry ingredients along with the walnuts. Mix well. Pour onto the base and sprinkle generously with the granulated sugar. Bake for 35 minutes or until it keeps its shape if pressed. Stand for 5 minutes before turning onto a wire rack to cool.

Variation: Jaffa Cake

Omit the nutmeg and walnuts and add the zest of an orange to the cake part. To make the filling, mix 200g / 7oz marmalade with 25g / 1oz sugar, zest of 1 orange and 1 tbs or more of orange juice to make it runny. Use this to make a layer of filling between the base and the cake. Don't sprinkle with sugar but once cool, spread the top with 85g / 3oz of very dark chocolate melted with 25g / 1oz of butter.

Banana Cake

Martin brought this recipe to Doune from a previous life. It is fantastic freshly baked for tea or coffee time and also packs well for an energy boost when walking. Dark chocolate drops make a great substitute for the dates if you want a change.

makes 18 pieces

160g / 5½oz butter, softened
250g / 9oz granulated sugar
3 eggs
4 bananas
275g / 10oz self-raising flour
½ tsp bicarbonate of soda
½ tsp salt
175g / 6oz chopped dates

Preheat the oven to 180°C / gas mark 4. Prepare a 30x23cm / 12x9in traybake tin by lining with silicon paper. Beat the butter and sugar together until light and fluffy. Skin and mash the bananas with a potato masher and add along with all the other ingredients. Mix gently and thoroughly. Pour into the prepared tin and bake for 45 minutes. Test by inserting a skewer or sharp knife into the middle of the cake, if it comes out clean it is done. Allow to cool for a few minutes then turn out onto a wire rack and remove the paper to cool completely.

Tea Loaf

This is a really lovely fruity and zingy tea loaf. Warning, you need to allow time to soak the fruit.

makes 1 loaf
350g / 12oz dried fruit (mostly raisins)
225g / 8oz self-raising flour
125g / 4½ oz demerara sugar
1 egg
1 tbs marmalade
grated rind 1 orange

Well cover the fruit in hot tea and soak for a minimum of 1½ hours or overnight. Preheat the oven to 190°C / gas mark 5. Prepare a standard 900g / 2lb loaf tin by lining with silicon paper. Drain the excess tea from the fruit and discard. Mix the fruit with all the rest of the ingredients and use to fill the tin. Bake for half an hour. Turn down the oven to 170°C / gas mark 3 and bake for a further hour or until an inserted skewer just barely comes out clean. (It is meant to be a bit sticky.) Cool in the tin.

Lemon Drizzle Cake

Our version of the classic lemon drizzle cake came from my mother in law.

makes 18
225g / 8oz softened butter
225g / 8oz caster sugar
zest 1½ lemons
4 eggs, beaten
225g / 8oz self-raising flour
for the drizzle:
85g / 3oz granulated sugar
juice 1½ lemons

Preheat the oven to 180°C / gas mark 4. Line a 30x23cm / 12x9in traybake tin with silicon paper. Beat the butter, caster sugar and lemon rind together until soft and fluffy. Mix in the egg and flour as gently as possible and pour into the tin. Bake for 30 minutes then reduce the oven temperature to 170°C / gas mark 3 and cook a further 10 minutes or until the cake bounces back when gently pressed. While it is still in the tin, prick the cooked cake all over with a fork. Mix the sugar and lemon juice and drizzle evenly over the top. Leave for a few minutes to soak in, then turn out on to a wire rack to finish cooling.

Variation:

Orange Drizzle Cake

Substitute oranges for the lemons.

Fruity Bran Cake

Based on a very old promotional recipe for All-Bran this is still really popular. We use a high proportion of currants along with sultanas, cranberries and mixed peel giving it a bit more zing than the standard shop dried fruit mix. It is ridiculously easy.

makes 1 loaf
110g / 4oz bran cereal
150g / 5oz sugar
280ml / ½ pint milk
110g / 4oz self-raising flour
350g / 12 oz mixed dried fruit

Preheat the oven to 180°C / gas mark 4. Prepare a standard 900g / 2lb loaf tin by lining with silicon paper. Soak the bran cereal in the milk for 30 minutes. Mix in everything else and pour into the prepared tin. Bake for 1 hour or until an inserted skewer comes out clean.

Malt Loaf

We have spent a long time trying to find the perfect malt loaf. Our original recipe was just a bit too vague to be consistently good. In the process, we have made many, (tough work but someone had to do it), and our final version is based on a lovely recipe by Felicity Cloake. It should be served sliced and buttered.

makes 1 loaf
150g / 5oz malt extract
85g / 3oz golden syrup
50g / 2oz black treacle
50g / 2oz soft brown sugar
150ml / 6 fl oz strong tea
200g / 7oz mixed dried fruit
125g / 4½ oz plain flour
125g / 4½ oz wholemeal flour
3 tsp baking powder
½ tsp salt

Preheat the oven to 180°C / gas mark 4. Prepare a standard 900g / 2lb loaf tin by lining with silicon paper. Put all the ingredients in a large bowl and mix together well. Bake, covering lightly with foil half way through, for about 50 minutes or until an inserted skewer just barely comes out clean. (It is meant to be a bit sticky.) Cool in the tin.

Courgette Chocolate Cake

The perfect way to use some of a glut of courgettes, either your own or if your neighbour has offloaded some of theirs on your doorstep. (On Knoydart, donors leave them anonymously in people's vehicles!) It is moist and rather delicate so we have stopped using it for packed lunches, but it makes a lovely teatime cake. For this, use a 23cm / 9in round tin, (it will take slightly longer to cook). If you want to ice it, use all the walnuts and chocolate chips in the main mixture and top with vanilla butter icing or the lime frosting given with the carrot cake recipe on page 154.

makes 18

150g / 5oz soft butter
175g / 6oz granulated sugar
175g / 6oz self-raising flour
pinch salt
1 tbs cocoa powder
1 egg
½ tsp vanilla essence
75ml / 3 fl oz milk
1 courgette, grated
40g / 1½ oz walnut pieces
110g / 4oz chocolate chips

Preheat the oven to 180°C / gas mark 4. Line a 30x23cm / 12x9in traybake tin with silicon paper. Cream the butter and sugar until light and fluffy. Sift together the flour, salt and cocoa powder. Beat the eggs with the vanilla and milk. Mix all together. Stir in the courgette and half the walnuts and chocolate chips. Pour into the tin and sprinkle with the rest of the walnuts and chocolate chips. Bake for 35 to 40 minutes until just done. Cool in the tin.

Ginger Cake

When I first came to the West Coast I worked in a café in Shieldaig called Ann's Parlour. This is their ginger-bread recipe which we are still using 38 years later!

makes 1 loaf

250g / 9oz black treacle
110g / 4oz butter
110g / 4oz sugar
275g / 10oz plain flour
1 level tsp bicarbonate of soda
2 level tsp ground ginger
1 level tsp ground cinnamon
1 egg, beaten
235ml / 8 fl oz milk
½ tsp vinegar

Preheat the oven to 170°C / gas mark 3. Prepare a standard 900g / 2lb loaf tin by lining with silicon paper. Weigh the treacle, butter and sugar into a pan and melt gently. Sieve the dry ingredients into a large bowl. Mix the melted ingredients into the dry and stir until properly mixed. Beat the egg, milk and vinegar together and add about a quarter to the bowl. Mix well, but be gentle, and then stir in the rest. When all incorporated it will be quite a runny batter. Pour it into the tin and bake for 1¼ to 1½ hours until an inserted skewer comes out clean. Let it settle for a few minutes then turn out and cool on a rack.

Carrot Cake

Most carrot cake recipes use oil but I prefer to substitute melted butter. I have used this recipe since the beginning but I don't remember where it came from. You can substitute half the flour with wholemeal plus ½ a teaspoon of baking powder. You can also add pumpkin or sunflower seeds or walnuts or all of them. We don't ice this cake for packing but the lime frosting is great for teatime.

makes 1 loaf
225g / 8oz self-raising flour
200g / 7oz soft brown sugar
60g / 2½ oz desiccated coconut
1 tsp ground cinnamon
2 carrots, grated
4 eggs
225g / 8oz butter, melted
<u>for the frosting:</u>
200g / 7oz cream cheese
zest and juice 1 lime
2 dsp light soft brown sugar

Preheat the oven to 180°C / gas mark 4. Prepare a standard 900g / 2lb loaf tin by lining with silicon paper. For the cake, combine the first 5 ingredients in a large bowl. Beat the eggs with the melted butter and mix gently into the dry ingredients. Turn into the tin and bake for about an hour until an inserted skewer comes out clean. Turn out onto a rack and remove the paper to cool. For the frosting, beat all the ingredients together and spread roughly on the top.

bread

Doune Bread Rolls

We make fresh bread every day of the season. Our recipe is quite idiosyncratic, but it achieves the result we are after; light, soft rolls, not too thick so they become impossible to eat once they are filled for packed lunches! As with all our recipes, our method has developed over time but the end result is still the same. We use a quick rise so that we can fit the process into our daily routine and 5.00 pm is bread-making time. We aim to have it baking as our guests arrive in the Dining Room for pre-dinner drinks. This is half of what we call our standard mix, when busy we will make up to 3 mixes at a time!

makes 20 rolls
350g / 12oz granary flour
350g / 12oz strong white bread flour
1 sachet easy blend dried yeast
1½ tsp salt
1½ tsp sugar
525ml / 18.5 fl oz warm water

Line two baking trays with silicon paper. Measure and warm the water so it is very warm to the touch but not scalding. Put all the dry ingredients in a large bowl and mix well. Add all the water and mix to a soft, rather sticky dough. Cover and leave in a warm place for about 20 minutes. Turn out onto a good sprinkling of flour and, using a bread scraper or long-bladed knife, move the dough from the outer edges to the centre. The outside of the dough should be floury but the inside still sticky. Now, with some flour on your hands, knead gently for about a minute or until the dough is just springy. You can sprinkle more flour if you want but try not to add any more to the mix, just use enough to prevent sticking. Divide and shape into rolls and place on the trays close enough so they will touch each other when risen. Leave to rise in a warm place for about 1½ hours. They should be well risen, so leave longer if required. Preheat the oven to 220°C / gas mark 8. Bake on the second shelf down, one tray at a time, for 8 to 10 minutes or until lightly browned. Once out of the oven, turn the rolls upside down and remove the paper. Cool like this for a few minutes before pulling the rolls apart and serving. For crustier rolls, place further apart and cook longer at a slightly lower temperature.

For our bread and fruit loaves, see page 156.

For **Bread Loaves** knead slightly longer, incorporating more flour as you go so the dough is not quite as sticky. This quantity will make two 900g / 2lb loaves. Cook as for Doune bread rolls for 10 minutes then reduce the temperature to 190°C / gas mark 5 for a further 10 to 15 minutes. A fully cooked loaf should be slightly coloured on the bottom and sound hollow if tapped. Remove from the tin and paper and cool on a rack.

We often serve **Fruit Loaves** as a breakfast extra. Pat our bread roll dough out to a rectangle about 0.8cm / ⅓ in thick. Sprinkle or spread on your filling, roll up and place in a tin to rise. Cook as for bread loaves. Filling ideas: Sultana and spice. Date and orange or walnut. Raspberry jam and coconut. Cinnamon and apple. Chocolate chip and coconut. Apricot and almond. Marmalade and chocolate chip. Marmalade, orange zest, mixed peel and sugar. Cinnamon and sugar, topped with icing. Prune, pistachio and brown sugar.

On Friday night before our prawn buffet, to ring the changes, we usually make **Bread Plaits** instead of rolls. A very slightly higher ratio of granary to white flour and a little less water than for the rolls plus shaping instead of using a tin (so giving more surface area) makes a beautiful, crusty, rustic loaf. Form into plaits or any shape you fancy and place on a lined tray. We usually brush with a little milk and sprinkle with mixed seeds and oatmeal. Cook as for bread loaves.

Gluten Free Bread

Right at the beginning, we realised a need to provide gluten free bread for coeliacs, and I managed to source this recipe and all the special flours required. (Not so easy before the internet!) It turned out to be very acceptable and even now with gluten free diets being so much more common, and products and recipes everywhere, I have not found anything better. It remains one of our most requested recipes. We use a 250ml cup.

makes 1 loaf
2 cups white rice flour
½ cup tapioca starch flour
½ cup potato starch flour
2 ½ tsp xanthan gum
Or instead of the four above:
3 cups gluten free bread flour

1 tsp salt
1 tsp sugar
1 sachet gluten free dried yeast
2 large eggs
¼ cup olive oil
½ cup milk or milk substitute
1 ¼ cups hot water

Line a 900g / 2lb loaf tin with silicon paper. Mix all the dry ingredients in a bowl. Beat together the eggs and the rest of the wet ingredients. Mix wet into dry, adding a little more water if needed to make a very thick batter, and beat until it is all smooth. It should leave a trail but be far too sticky to attempt to knead like normal bread. Pour into the tin and roughly spread flat. Rise in a warm place until it fills the tin. (It will be quite wobbly.) Preheat the oven to 200°C / gas mark 6. Bake for 30 to 40 minutes until nicely browned, turn out, remove the paper and cool on a rack. It is best eaten fresh. Slice and freeze any excess straight away. Slices will defrost in about an hour and can then be reheated in foil for about 5 minutes in a moderate oven.

Gluten Free Recipes

Just as the ready mixed gluten-free bread flour has made making gluten free bread so much easier so the other gluten free flour mixes mean you can bake pretty much anything. There are plenty of specialist books and recipes out there so rather than give recipes here I am just going to mention a few tips that might help when substituting gluten free flour for wheat.

1. All the replacement flours seem to soak up more moisture than wheat flour does, so if your mixture seems dry, do add a little more liquid, water is fine. For cakes you need a soft mixture that falls off the spoon easily. For pastry make a sticky dough then wrap it and leave it in the fridge for 30 minutes to absorb the water before trying to roll it out.

2. If you have added more liquid you may need to increase the cooking time a little.

3. Texture and flavour will be improved if you have some extra protein in the mix such as egg, milk or ground almonds.

4. For mixtures that need to hold air to make them light, you will need xanthan gum. It is included in bread mixes but if you are making your own mix you will need to add 2 teaspoons to every 225g / 8oz. We have made very successful choux pastry this way. For cakes, 1 tsp per 225g / 8oz will do the trick. Self raising gluten free flours will include it already. The gum comes as fine granules; always add it to the dry ingredients before mixing.

5. For pastry and shortbread I also find a little xanthan gum helps to keep it from being too crumbly. A good pinch in 225g / 8oz is enough or you can substitute a little of the flour with a bread flour mix. Go carefully though, too much will make it hard, especially if kept for a few days.

6. Gluten free baking powder is now freely available. I have noticed that it can have a stronger bicarb. taste, so be careful not to be over generous.

Garlic Croissant

Doune prawn night wouldn't be the same without our home-made garlic croissant. It all started on the opening night in the Dining Room with a giant platter of prawns and Mary deciding they should be served with garlic croissant. We have changed the recipe and method a few times over the years and have currently settled on the following as being the best and easiest yet. If you think rolling the butter is too long winded another way is to grate chilled butter onto the dough. This recipe makes a lot but they freeze well, baked or unbaked. Baked ones benefit from a quick freshening up in the oven for a few minutes. If freezing unbaked, do so straight away; they are best properly defrosted before baking.

makes 20
315ml / 11 fl oz really cold water to mix
225g / 8oz good quality butter
450g / 1lb strong white flour
1 sachet dried easy blend yeast
2 tsp salt
beaten egg to brush
8 medium garlic cloves, crushed

Refrigerate the water. Flatten the butter between two sheets of greaseproof paper so that it is about 25x12.5cm / 10x5in and leave in the fridge. Line your oven tray(s) with silicon paper. Mix the flour, yeast, salt and the cold water to make a stiff dough. Knead to bring it together and roll out so it is just over twice as big as the butter. Place the butter on one side and fold the rest over to cover it, seal the edges around the butter really well. Now roll into a very long oblong. Fold the short edges in so they meet in the middle and then fold in half along the line where they meet. This is called a book fold. Turn through 90° and roll and book fold again. Place in a plastic bag and leave to rest in the fridge for a minimum of half an hour. Remove and roll and book fold. Rest again. Roll to an oblong about 0.65cm / ¼ in thick. With a very sharp knife or pizza cutter, cut the thinnest strip possible around the edges and discard. Cut the dough into long triangles. Spread a little garlic on to each and brush the tips of the triangles with a little egg. Give the middle of the short end of the triangles (opposite the tips) a small cut. Pull these ends apart slightly to make them longer and roll up towards the tip of the triangles. Bend each into a crescent shape, and put on the oven trays with the tip underneath. Brush with more egg and leave to rest (not too hot a place or the butter starts to melt) for about half an hour. Bake in the middle of a preheated oven at 220°C / gas mark 7 for about 12 minutes until crisp and golden. If cooking two trays they are best baked separately. Remove to a rack to cool a little, serve warm.

Variation: Danish Pastries

We use the same recipe to make mini Danish pastries for breakfast. Use whatever size or shape you fancy. For **sweet croissant**, you can add 50g / 2oz sugar to the mix and sprinkle with a little sugar before baking. Filling ideas include **raspberry jam**, **almond paste, chocolate,** and **walnut with maple syrup and cinnamon.** Glaze with syrup or icing and sprinkle with nuts as you like.

Shortbread

We always put some home baking in the rooms for our guests on arrival. We call it 'Welcome Cake' but it is invariably shortbread and many folk have said it is the best shortbread they have ever had. The recipe came from a friend's granny and is delicious and incredibly easy. For optimum results, do use the best quality butter you can.

makes 12 pieces
275g / 10oz plain flour
25g / 1oz ground rice
25g / 1oz cornflour
225g / 8oz cold butter
110g / 4oz caster sugar
sugar for sprinkling

Preheat the oven to 160°C / gas mark 2 to 3. Line a 30x23cm / 12x9in traybake tin with silicon paper. The easiest way to make this is to use a food processor but if you don't have one rubbing it in the old-fashioned way works fine. Either way, everything goes in together and is either processed or rubbed in until it makes very fine 'crumbs' which are just beginning to stick together. Press into the tin and smooth down without too much pressure using the back of a metal spoon. Bake for 10 minutes, remove, prick all over with a fork and return to the oven for another hour or so until slightly coloured. When done, immediately sprinkle with a little more sugar and leave to settle for just a few minutes. Cut and remove while still warm and finish cooling on a wire rack.

Variation: Petticoat Shortbread

We often serve these with Old Fashioned Posset (page 95) or our home-made ice creams (page 104). Beat 110g / 4oz of soft butter with 50g / 2oz caster sugar until soft and fluffy. Mix in 175g / 6oz plain flour, wrap and chill for about 15 minutes. Divide the dough into two, roll each into a round and cut into 6 or 8 triangles. Bake at 180°C / gas mark 4 for 15 to 20 minutes until starting to brown at the edges. Sprinkle with a little more sugar. Allow to cool on the tray for a few minutes before removing to a rack.

pastry

With all pastry, the quicker you can work, the better the result. Use quick, decisive strokes of the rolling pin. The pastry knows if you are frightened of it!

Puff Pastry

The high gluten content of the strong flour gives strength to the layers and helps the rise. Good quality butter has fewer impurities and will give a better result. It is a good idea to refrigerate some water an hour or so before you start.

for a 6 person pie
175g / 6oz cold butter
175g / 6oz strong white flour
a good pinch of salt
very cold water to mix

Flatten 150g / 5oz of the butter between two sheets of greaseproof paper and chill. Grate the rest into the flour and salt. Mix in enough water so that all the flour is mixed in. It should be soft but not sticky. Turn onto a floured surface and knead until smooth. Roll into an oblong just over twice the size of the butter. Place the flattened butter onto one side, fold the rest over it and seal the edges. Now, with a little flour on the surface and rolling pin to avoid sticking, roll into a very long oblong, keeping rolling strokes inwards and avoiding rolling off the edges so keeping the air bubbles in. It should be quite thin. Fold the short edges in so they meet in the middle and then fold in half along the line where they meet. This is called a book fold. Place in a plastic bag and leave to rest in the fridge for a minimum of half an hour, longer if you can. Remove, turn through 90° and using the same technique, roll and book fold again. Rest again and repeat. Rest again and roll out to the shape required. Make sure you have a cut edge all around and glaze with egg or milk. Puff pastry should be baked on the middle shelf of the oven so that the heat from the roof of the oven doesn't cook the top too fast and stop the rise. Use a preheated oven at 220°C / gas mark 7 and bake for 20 to 25 minutes until golden brown and crisp.

Shortcrust Pastry

Too much liquid is what makes shortcrust pastry tough (along with excess handling). We use a higher ratio of fat to flour which helps it stick together without too much water. Adding an egg yolk would be another way. Using a food processor makes a smooth dough with a short and crumbly finish which suits our tart recipes. Rubbing in by hand is likely to produce a lighter result and, in this case, I would suggest using baking beans for baking blind as it is more prone to rising. This quantity is exactly right for the tin; if you are unused to rolling pastry, allow a little more.

to line a 25.5cm / 10in shallow tart tin
175g / 6oz plain flour
100g / 3½ oz butter, at room temperature
3 drops of cold water
1 dsp caster sugar (optional for sweet recipes)

Process the flour and butter to resemble fine crumbs. Mix in the sugar if you are wanting a sweet pastry. Add the water and process to form a dough. (You can add more if you find it difficult to handle, but keep it to as little as possible.) If it is very soft, wrap and chill for a few minutes but not too long as this will make it too firm to roll easily. Working as quickly as possible, roll and shape as needed using flour to avoid sticking. Use short brisk strokes and try to keep it in the shape you want by pushing it back with your hands. Carefully roll it onto your rolling pin to transfer it to the tin. Try not to stretch it to make it fit, ease it in, pushing rather than pulling. Lay any excess over the sides and cut it off by pressing down on top with the rolling pin. To bake blind, bake in a preheated oven 180°C / gas mark 4 for 20 minutes until starting to colour. To produce a crisper finish we find it better not to use paper and baking beans. Neither do we prick the pastry.

Flaky Pastry

This will be flaky and crumbly but won't have the rise and layers of puff pastry.

for a 6 person pie
225g / 8oz plain four
175g / 6oz chilled butter
a good pinch of salt
very cold water to mix

The butter should be very well chilled and it is best put into the freezer for half an hour. Put the flour and salt into a large bowl and coarsely grate the butter into the flour. Mix well with a knife until the butter bits are coated with flour. Sprinkle in 4 to 6 tablespoons of cold water and mix to bring together, finishing off with your hands. Wrap and chill for 30 minutes. When rolled and cut into shape(s), knock the edges with the back of a knife to give a flaky edge. Glaze with egg or milk, and bake in a preheated oven at 220°C / gas mark 7 for about 20 minutes.

Choux Pastry

A combination of flours gives the best results, the strong providing a framework for a big rise and light result and the plain keeping a soft texture. You can use all of either type if you need to. A food mixer is great for the beating stage.

serves 6

25g / 1oz butter
140ml / ¼ pint water
pinch salt
70g / 2½ oz plain flour, sieved
70g / 2½ oz strong flour, sieved
2 eggs, beaten

Melt the butter gently, add the water and pinch of salt and bring to the boil. When boiling fast add all the flour and beat over the heat with a wooden spoon until it makes a thick paste and all the flour is mixed in properly, with no lumps. Reduce the heat and cook gently, stirring all the time for about a minute. Remove from the heat, and beat hard to cool slightly. Add the egg a bit at a time, beating vigorously. When nearly all the egg is in, check the consistency as you may or may not need it all. The paste needs to be soft and smooth but not so soft that it spreads; it must hold its shape. Too much egg and it goes splat, too little and it doesn't rise very well and is heavy and gooey. Spoon or pipe the paste onto a lined baking tray into the shapes you want. Bake in the middle of a preheated of oven at 200°C / gas mark 6 for 20 to 25 minutes. Reduce the heat to 180°C / gas mark 4, and cook for a further 5 minutes. Prick each shape with a sharp knife to let out the steam and return to the oven for 5 more minutes. They should be quite crisp, but on the other hand you don't want them too hard. Cool on a rack and cover with a clean tea towel until required. If not using on the day, keep in an airtight tin.

thanks

2019 will be the 25th season of Doune Dining Room and this book is a way of celebrating my journey and love affair with the Doune kitchen.
First of all, thank you to Alan and Mary who first came to Doune in 1981 with their sons Toby and Jamie and started the whole thing off. Andy and I joined them in 1991 and, in spring 1994, the Dining Room was born.
Following on, huge thanks to Martin and Jane who took over the Dining Room in 2003, and nurtured it to grow and develop into the success it is today.
Thanks also to all the amazing people who have worked with us; every year is different and an inspiration.
And, of course, thank you to all our fantastic guests, without you all, there wouldn't be a Doune.

Special thanks to my good friend Ann for proofreading, to Daniel, our printer, who answered endless questions, and to Andy who has prepared all the photographs and may have put up with a little extra stress at home this year!

Slàinte, Liz

stats

Just for fun we have done a few approximate calculations and in twenty five years the Doune kitchen has seen its fair share of action....

1,400 large tarts baked
70,000 Doune eggs cooked for breakfasts (poor chickens!)
75 litres of chutney made
2,100 marmalade oranges processed
284,375 bread rolls baked

index